# Puzzle Baron's

# KIDS' PUZZLES

## ALPHA

A member of Penguin Random House LLC

**Publisher:** Mike Sanders
**Associate Publisher:** Billy Fields
**Acquisitions Editor:** Jan Lynn
**Cover/Book Designer:** Kurt Owens
**Compositor:** Ayanna Lacey
**Proofreader:** Jamie Fields

First American Edition, 2017
Published in the United States by DK Publishing
6081 E. 82nd Street, Indianapolis, Indiana 46250

ISBN: 9781465464842

# CONTENTS

# INTRODUCTION

Do you love to solve puzzles? If so, you've picked the right book!
We've got more than 300 puzzles and brain teasers here ready to
be solved. Word games, math puzzles, logic puzzles, mazes, Sudoku,
dot-to-dots ... you name it, we've got it! Puzzle Baron's Kids' Puzzles
is guaranteed to keep you entertained for hours and hours. And who
knows, you might even learn a few things along the way!

If you've enjoyed these puzzles, check out our online games and
mobile applications at our website: http://www.puzzlebaron.com.

The illustrations in this book were done by Joe Wos, a cartoonist,
illustrator, and maze-maker from Pennsylvania. You can find more
of his work, including links to lots more of his fun illustrated mazes,
at his website: http://mazetoons.wixsite.com/wosisme

# ACROSTICS

Mini acrostic puzzles are like a mix between a cryptogram and a traditional crossword puzzle. Solve the crossword clues to gradually fill in letters in the hidden quote. As the quote begins to emerge, it will provide you with letters for the clues you've not yet solved. Work the puzzle back and forth between the clues and the quote until you've revealed the solution!

# PUZZLE #1

| 1 | 2 | 3 | 4 | ■ | 5 | 6 | 7 | 8 | 9 | 10 | ■ | 11 | 12 | ■ |
|---|---|---|---|---|---|---|---|---|---|----|----|----|----|----|
| 13 | 14 | 15 | ■ | 16 | 17 | 18 | 19 | ■ | 20 | 21 | 22 | 23 | 24 | 25 |
| 26 | 27 | 28 | ■ | 29 | 30 | 31 | 32 | 33 | ■ | 34 | 35 | 36 | 37 | ■ |

| 18 | 6 | 5 | 26 | 3 |
|----|---|---|----|---|

Not flexible at all

| 1 | 2 | 21 | 22 |
|---|---|----|----|

Simba or Nala

| 34 | 17 | 20 | 4 | 9 |
|----|----|----|---|---|

You dry your hands with it

| 29 | 31 | 10 | 19 | 33 |
|----|----|----|----|----|

Half of one hundred

| 25 | 27 | 36 | 8 | 32 |
|----|----|----|---|----|

Measuring tool

| 14 | 11 | 23 | 37 |
|----|----|----|----|

_____ and seek (game)

| 16 | 15 | 13 | 35 | 28 |
|----|----|----|----|----|

Copper, gold, or iron

| 12 | 24 | 30 | 7 |
|----|----|----|---|

Sail the seven _____

# PUZZLE #2

| 1 | 2 | 3 | ■ | 4 | 5 | 6 | ■ | 7 | 8 | ■ | 9 | 10 | 11 | 12 |
|---|---|---|---|---|---|---|---|---|---|---|---|---|---|---|
| ■ | 13 | 14 | 15 | ■ | 16 | 17 | 18 | 19 | ■ | 20 | 21 | 22 | 23 | ■ |
| 24 | 25 | ■ | 26 | 27 | 28 | 29 | 30 | ■ | 31 | 32 | 33 | ? | | |

<u>   </u> <u>   </u> <u>   </u> <u>   </u> <u>   </u>
4   21   22   27   3

Eight times five

<u>   </u> <u>   </u> <u>   </u> <u>   </u> <u>   </u> <u>   </u>
6   1   17   8   33   13

Half of the previous answer

<u>   </u> <u>   </u> <u>   </u>
16   14   9

Exclamation of amazement

<u>   </u> <u>   </u> <u>   </u> <u>   </u>
20   15   26   10

"Here we go round the mulberry _____"

<u>   </u> <u>   </u> <u>   </u> <u>   </u> <u>   </u> <u>   </u>
18   32   7   12   11   30

Destroyed

<u>   </u> <u>   </u> <u>   </u> <u>   </u> <u>   </u>
25   23   5   31   29

Vegetable that can make you cry

<u>   </u> <u>   </u> <u>   </u> <u>   </u>
2   19   28   24

Make warmer

# PUZZLE #3

| 1 | 2 | | 3 | 4 | 5 | 6 | 7 | | ! | 8 | | 9 | 10 | 11 | 12 |
|---|---|---|---|---|---|---|---|---|---|---|---|---|---|---|---|
| 13 | 14 | | 15 | 16 | 17 | | 18 | 19 | 20 | 21 | 22 | 23 | | 24 | |
| 25 | 26 | | 27 | 28 | | | | 29 | 30 | | 31 | 32 | 33 | 34 | |
| | 35 | 36 | | 37 | 38 | 39 | | 40 | 41 | 42 | ! | 43 | | 44 | |
| 45 | 46 | 47 | ! | | | | | | | | | | | | |

---

| 9 | 46 | 7 | 28 | 47 | 20 | 31 | 24 |
Board game with tiny hotels

| 34 | 14 | 10 | 40 | 26 | 35 | 11 | 5 |
Finish school and earn a diploma

| 18 | 42 | 4 | 17 |
Frosty the _____ Man

| 27 | 32 | 25 | 30 | 13 |
"Duck, duck, _____!"

| 36 | 45 | 39 | 3 | 23 |
Prepare for an exam

| 16 | 21 | 22 | 6 |
Hogwarts messenger birds

| 15 | 41 | 38 | 8 |
Sound made by previous answer

| 33 | 29 | 44 | 43 | 37 |
Very unpleasant

| 12 | 1 | 19 | 2 |
Lean just a bit

**4    Puzzle Baron's Kids' Puzzles**

# PUZZLE #4

| 1 | 2 | 3 | 4 | 5 | | 6 | 7 | 8 | | 9 | 10 | 11 | 12 | 13 |
|---|---|---|---|---|---|---|---|---|---|---|----|----|----|----|
| 14 | 15 | | 16 | 17 | 18 | | | 19 | 20 | 21 | 22 | | 23 | 24 |
| 25 | | 26 | 27 | 28 | | 29 | 30 | | 31 | 32 | 33 | 34 | | 35 |
| 36 | 37 | 38 | | | | | | | | | | | | |

___ ___ ___ ___ ___
26  18  19  9  23

Disney dog who says "ah-hyuck!"

___ ___ ___ ___
31  20  2  12

"I _____ it was you!"

___ ___ ___ ___ ___
28  14  13  22  5

What apples grow on

___ ___ ___
21  30  34

It goes "moo"

___ ___ ___ ___ ___
38  11  25  15  3

Mickey _____

___ ___ ___ ___
16  17  1  32

Place smaller than a city

___ ___ ___ ___
36  8  37  10

Back part of the foot

___ ___ ___ ___
35  24  6  4

Frog-like animal

___ ___ ___ ___
29  33  7  27

Ripped some paper

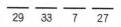

# PUZZLE #5

| 1 | 2 | | 3 | 4 | 5 | | 6 | 7 | | 8 | 9 | 10 | 11 | 12 |
|---|---|---|---|---|---|---|---|---|---|---|---|---|---|---|
| 13 | 14 | 15 | | 16 | 17 | | 18 | 19 | 20 | 21 | 22 | 23 | | |
| 24 | 25 | 26 | 27 | 28 | 29 | 30 | 31 | , | | 32 | 33 | | 34 | |
| 35 | 36 | 37 | 38 | 39 | 40 | 41 | 42 | 43 | . | | | | | |

—— —— —— —— —— ——
28  17  12  5  24  33

April, May, and June

—— —— —— ——
38  6  37  18

The early bird gets the _____

—— —— —— —— ——
26  23  9  40  41

Place to wear a watch

—— —— —— ——
1  3  32  30

What a hammer hits

—— —— —— —— —— —— —— —— ——
14  22  35  36  16  21  13  42  10

Eight plus nine

—— —— ——
25  11  43

Opposite of even

—— —— —— ——
4  39  20  27

Lions and tigers (but not bears)

—— —— —— ——
31  34  19  7

Tree part that falls in Autumn

—— —— —— ——
15  2  29  8

Make very, very wet

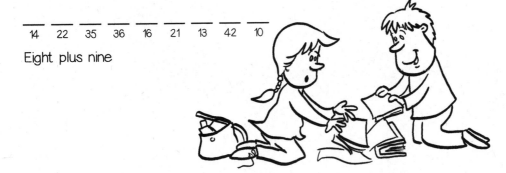

# PUZZLE #6

| 1 | | 2 | 3 | 4 | 5 | 6 | 7 | 8 | | 9 | 10 | | 11 | |
|---|---|---|---|---|---|---|---|---|---|---|---|---|---|---|
| 12 | 13 | 14 | 15 | 16 | 17 | 18 | 19 | | 20 | 21 | 22 | 23 | 24 | |
| 25 | 26 | 27 | 28 | 29 | 30 | | 31 | 32 | 33 | 34 | | 35 | | 36 |
| 37 | 38 | 39 | 40 | 41 | | 42 | 43 | 44 | 45 | | | | | |

‾25‾ ‾23‾ ‾17‾ ‾4‾ ‾33‾ ‾8‾

_____ and the Beast

‾2‾ ‾21‾ ‾27‾ ‾42‾ ‾1‾ ‾31‾

Type of puzzle

‾24‾ ‾45‾ ‾9‾ ‾14‾ ‾29‾

"... dish ran away with the _____"

‾18‾ ‾44‾ ‾16‾ ‾12‾

Baby bird's home

‾20‾ ‾3‾ ‾15‾ ‾38‾ ‾43‾ ‾11‾ ‾37‾ ‾6‾

Everest, for example

‾10‾ ‾35‾ ‾22‾ ‾40‾

It comes before winter

‾36‾ ‾7‾ ‾26‾ ‾19‾

Brown bit in a watermelon

‾5‾ ‾32‾ ‾30‾ ‾41‾

What the sun does in the morning

‾13‾ ‾28‾ ‾39‾ ‾34‾

Opposite of low

# PUZZLE #7

| 1 | 2 | 3 | ■ | 4 | 5 | 6 | 7 | ■ | 8 | 9 | 10 | 11 | 12 | 13 |
|---|---|---|---|---|---|---|---|---|---|---|----|----|----|----|
| 14 | 15 | 16 | ■ | 17 | 18 | 19 | 20 | 21 | 22 | 23 | 24 | 25 | 26 | ■ |
| 27 | 28 | 29 | ■ | 30 | 31 | 32 | ■ | 33 | 34 | 35 | 36 | 37 | ■ | 38 |
| 39 | ■ | 40 | 41 | ■ | 42 | 43 | ■ | 44 | 45 | 46 | 47 | ■ | | |

```
 6   38   20   46   12
_____ as sugar

 9   17   24   1   34
Our planet

 36   16   39   29   19   25
Jacket arm section

 8   13   47   3
Two-wheeled transport

 43   23   42
Opposite of in
```

```
 40   11   10   28   18
Word with security or dog

 33   45   44   22
School exam

 7   41   5   32   2
_____ fairy (pillow checker)

 15   30   26   27   14   37
Dangerous

 4   31   35   21
The cow jumped over the _____
```

# PUZZLE #8

| 1 | 2 | 3 | | 4 | 5 | 6 | 7 | | 8 | 9 | 10 | | 11 | 12 |
|---|---|---|---|---|---|---|---|---|---|---|----|----|----|----|
| | 13 | 14 | 15 | 16 | | 17 | | 18 | 19 | 20 | 21 | 22 | 23 | |
| 24 | 25 | | 26 | 27 | | 28 | 29 | | 30 | 31 | 32 | | | |

| 2 | 30 | 22 | 16 | 7 |
|---|---|---|---|---|

Sweet beehive product

| 6 | 29 | 18 | 26 |
|---|---|---|---|

Opposite of right

| 25 | 13 | 27 | 8 |
|---|---|---|---|

_____ and tell

| 15 | 24 | 23 | 21 | 4 |
|---|---|---|---|---|

Youtube offering

| 28 | 12 | 14 | 1 |
|---|---|---|---|

Water craft

| 5 | 20 | 31 | 3 | 11 | 10 |
|---|---|---|---|---|---|

Degrees in a right angle

| 17 | 19 | 32 | 9 |
|---|---|---|---|

_____ code (phone number part)

# PUZZLE #9

| 1 | | 2 | 3 | 4 | 5 | 6 | 7 | | 8 | 9 | 10 | | 11 | 12 |
|---|---|---|---|---|---|---|---|---|---|---|----|---|----|----|
| 13 | | 14 | 15 | 16 | 17 | | 18 | 19 | 20 | 21 | 22 | 23 | 24 | 25 |
| | 26 | 27 | 28 | 29 | 30 | 31 | | 32 | 33 | 34 | 35 | | 36 | 37 |
| | 38 | 39 | 40 | 41 | | | | | | | | | | |

$\overline{32}\ \overline{39}\ \overline{14}\ \overline{5}$

Birds lay them

$\overline{36}\ \overline{27}\ \overline{7}\ \overline{12}\ \overline{29}\ \overline{1}$

Yellow fruit

$\overline{2}\ \overline{16}\ \overline{30}\ \overline{23}$

Winnie the _____

$\overline{24}\ \overline{9}\ \overline{20}\ \overline{35}\ \overline{28}$

Prickly part of a rose

$\overline{11}\ \overline{10}\ \overline{21}\ \overline{4}$

60 minutes

$\overline{33}\ \overline{6}\ \overline{8}\ \overline{3}\ \overline{40}\ \overline{13}$

A, E, I, O, and U

$\overline{18}\ \overline{19}\ \overline{34}\ \overline{41}$

"... the harder _____ fall"

$\overline{26}\ \overline{38}\ \overline{31}\ \overline{37}$

Adorable

$\overline{17}\ \overline{15}\ \overline{22}\ \overline{25}$

Collies and poodles

# PUZZLE #10

| 1 | 2 | 3 | | 4 | 5 | 6 | 7 | 8 | 9 | | 10 | 11 | | 12 |
|---|---|---|---|---|---|---|---|---|---|---|---|---|---|---|
| 13 | 14 | 15 | 16 | 17 | 18 | | 19 | 20 | 21 | 22 | 23 | | 24 | 25 |
| | 26 | 27 | 28 | 29 | 30 | 31 | 32 | | 33 | 34 | 35 | 36 | 37 | 38 |
| 39 | | | | | | | | | | | | | | |

| 27 | 16 | 32 | 2 | 37 | 13 | 5 | 17 |
|----|----|----|---|----|----|---|----|

Six times three

| 15 | 24 | 26 | 20 | 9 |
|----|----|----|----|---|

Not loose

| 12 | 7 | 22 | 23 | 38 |
|----|---|----|----|----|

Report card mark

| 25 | 1 | 30 | 31 | 18 |
|----|---|----|----|----|

What angry bees do

| 8 | 19 | 4 | 29 |
|---|----|---|----|

Opposite of west

| 11 | 21 | 3 | 34 |
|----|----|---|----|

They go into shoes

| 6 | 35 | 36 | 39 |
|---|----|----|----|

One of 52 in a deck

| 28 | 10 | 14 | 33 |
|----|----|----|----|

Tater _____

# BUTTERFLY
# MATH

Each butterfly in these puzzles represents a different number. Can you use your math and logic skills to uncover each one?

# PUZZLE #1

🦋 + 🦋 = 10     🦋 = \_\_\_

🦋 x 🦋 = 10     🦋 = \_\_\_

🦋 + 🦋 = 🦋     🦋 = \_\_\_

# PUZZLE #2

🦋 x 🦋 = 12     🦋 = \_\_\_

🦋 - 🦋 = 1     🦋 = \_\_\_

🦋 x 🦋 = 🦋     🦋 = \_\_\_

## PUZZLE #3

🦋 + 🦋 + 🦋 = 21          🦋 = ___

🦋 + 🦋 + 🦋 = 13          🦋 = ___

🦋 − 🦋 = 3          🦋 = ___

🦋 + 🦋 + 🦋 = 🦋          🦋 = ___

## PUZZLE #4

🦋 x 🦋 x 🦋 = 27          🦋 = ___

🦋 x 🦋 x 🦋 = 6          🦋 = ___

🦋 + 🦋 = 5          🦋 = ___

🦋 + 🦋 + 🦋 = 🦋          🦋 = ___

# PUZZLE #5

 +  +  =          = ___

 ÷  = 2         = ___

 +  +  = 17         = ___

 -  - 2 =          = ___

# CLUELESS
# CROSSWORDS

Every number in the grid below corresponds to one particular letter. We've started you off by revealing several number-letter combinations. Can you complete the grid using only common, everyday words and place names? Hint: every letter from A to Z is used at least once!

# PUZZLE #1

Solution Grid:

| | | |
|---|---|---|
| 1 T | 2 | 3 |
| 4 D | 5 | 6 |
| 7 R | 8 | 9 |
| 10 I | 11 | 12 |
| 13 | 14 | 15 |
| 16 | 17 | 18 S |
| 19 | 20 J | 21 |
| 22 | 23 | 24 E |
| 25 | 26 U | |

A B C Ø Ɇ F G H Ɬ
Ø K L M N O P Q Ʀ
$ Ŧ Ʉ V W X Y Z

**FUN FACT**

Because of the Moon's slow erosion rate, footprints left there by astronauts will likely remain unchanged for up to 100 million years!

# PUZZLE #2

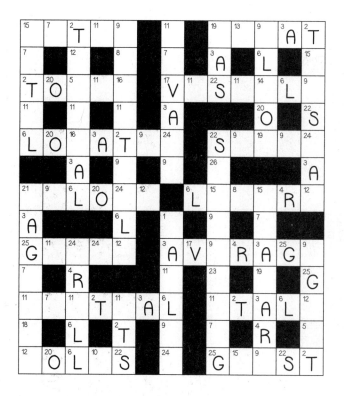

Solution Grid:

| 1 | 2 T | 3 A |
|---|---|---|
| 4 R | 5 | 6 L |
| 7 | 8 | 9 |
| 10 | 11 | 12 |
| 13 | 14 | 15 |
| 16 | 17 V | 18 |
| 19 | 20 O | 21 |
| 22 S | 23 | 24 |
| 25 G | 26 | |

A B C D E F G H I

J K L M N O P Q R

S T U V W X Y Z

# PUZZLE #3

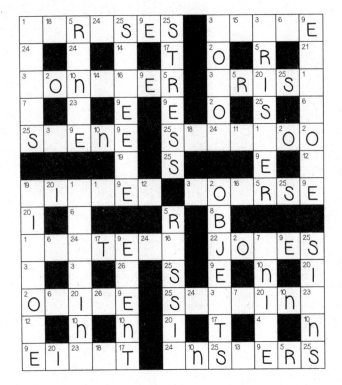

Solution Grid:

| 1 O | 2 O | 3 |
|---|---|---|
| 4 | 5 R | 6 |
| 7 | 8 B | E |
| 10 n | 11 | 12 |
| 13 | 14 | 15 |
| 16 | 17 T | 18 |
| 19 | 20 I | 21 |
| 22 J | 23 | 24 |
| 25 S | 26 | |

A B̸ C D E̸ F G H I̸

J̸ K L M N̸ O̸ P Q R̸

S̸ T̸ U V W X Y Z

# PUZZLE #4

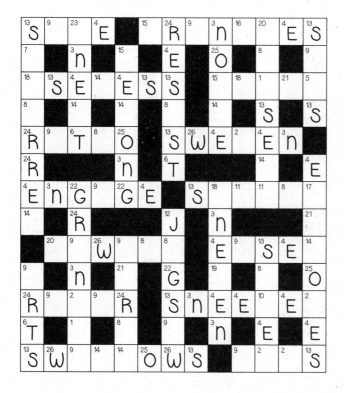

Solution Grid:

| 1 | 2 | 3 n |
| 4 E | 5 | 6 T |
| 7 | 8 | 9 |
| 10 | 11 | 12 J |
| 13 S | 14 | 15 |
| 16 | 17 | 18 |
| 19 | 20 | 21 |
| 22 G | 23 | 24 R |
| 25 O | 26 W | |

A B C D E̸ F G̸ H I

J̸ K L M N̸ O̸ P Q R̸

S̸ T̸ U V W̸ X Y Z

## Riddle

**HOW MANY MONTHS HAVE 28 DAYS?**

All of them

# PUZZLE #5

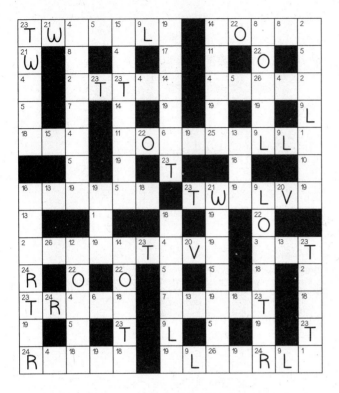

Solution Grid:

| | | |
|---|---|---|
| 1 | 2 | 3 |
| 4 | 5 | 6 |
| 7 | 8 | 9 L |
| 10 | 11 | 12 |
| 13 | 14 | 15 |
| 16 | 17 | 18 |
| 19 V | 20 W | 21 |
| 22 O | 23 T | 24 R |
| 25 | 26 | |

A B C D E F G H I

J K L M N O P Q R

S T U V W X Y Z

# CRAZY CODES

How good are you at distinguishing codes and symbols? See how you fare with the following seven Crazy Codes puzzles, each of which will require you to discern small differences between multiple symbols printed together on one page.

# PUZZLE #1

## ANCIENT SYMBOLS

Professor Parvin just discovered a bizarre series of ancient symbols painted on a cave wall on the island of Taveros! Help him translate the painting by finding the one and only symbol that is repeated FIVE times (and only five times) in the series below.

# PUZZLE #2

## COUNT THE SHAPES

There are five different shapes on this page: circles, squares, triangles, pentagons (with five sides), and hexagons (with six sides). Which of these shapes appears most frequently?

# PUZZLE #3

## UNIQUE SHAPES

Can you figure out how many unique shapes are on this page?

# PUZZLE #4

## ALIENS

How many different aliens can you find on this page? And which one appears only once.

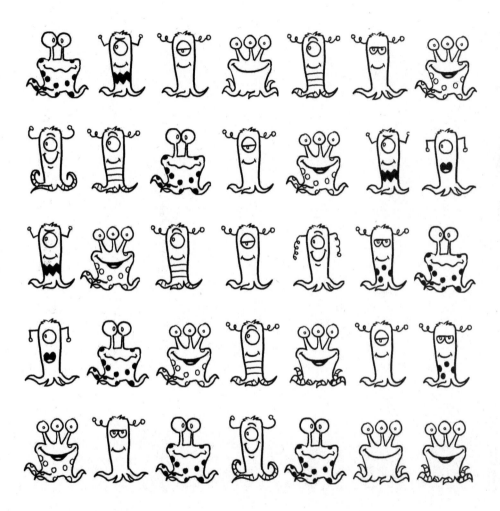

# PUZZLE #5

## CATS

Did you know a group of cats is called a "clowder"? See how many different kinds of cats you can find in this clowder, and figure out which type of cat appears the fewest times.

# PUZZLE #6

## FLOWERS

On this page there are eight different combinations of flowers and flowerpots. Each combination is slightly different. Can you find the one combination of flower and flowerpot which appears most frequently?

# PUZZLE #7

## ROBOTS

The latest batch of robots just arrived from the assembly plant, but you've been warned that one type of robot that shouldn't be in there snuck his way in! Can you find the only robot that appears once on this page?

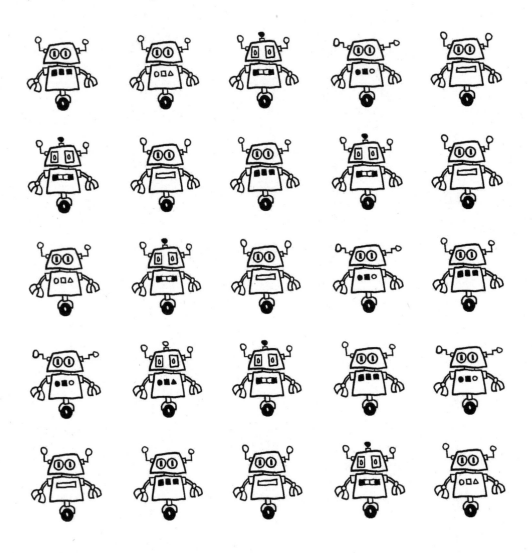

# CROSSWORDS

See if you can complete each of the following 10 crossword puzzles by filling in the grid with the clues and answers given. Each puzzle has one, and only one, unique solution. Good luck!

# PUZZLE #1

## CROSSED WORDS

Can you fit the following list of fruits into the grid? We've given you a head-start with CANTALOUPE ... now *see* if you can place the rest! Use each word only once, one letter per square.

| | |
|---|---|
| Apple | Orange |
| Banana | Peach |
| Cherry | Pear |
| Lemon | Plum |
| Lime | Watermelon |

# PUZZLE #2

## NUMBER CROSS

All of the answers in the grid below are whole numbers—spelled out as words—between one and ninety. Start with #4 Across, and see if you can fill in the entire grid using just the clues given and a bit of logic. No number will be used more than once. Good luck!

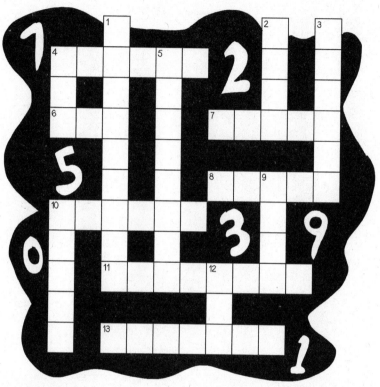

**Across**

**4.** 2 x 2 x 5

**6.** Less than 4 Down

**7.** 4 Down + 6 Across

**8.** More than 4 Across

**10.** Less than 5 Down

**11.** 5 Down + 9 Down + 1

**13.** 3 Down - 4 Across

**Down**

**1.** Less than 11 Across

**2.** Less than 9 Down

**3.** 8 Across + (10 Down x 9 Down)

**4.** Less than 7 Across

**5.** Less than 4 Across

**9.** More than 2 Down

**10.** Less than 5 Down

**12.** 10 Across - 6 Across

# PUZZLE #3

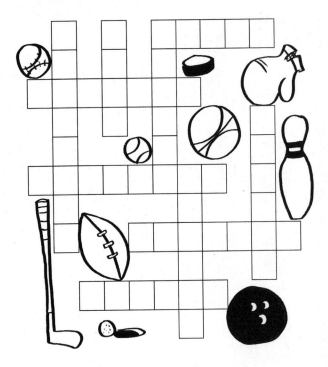

Bowling

Boxing

Cycling

Football

Golf

Hockey

Lacrosse

Soccer

Tennis

Track

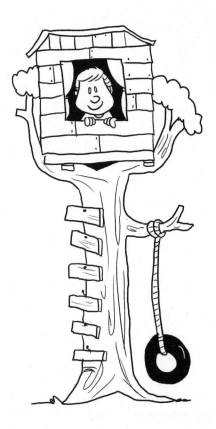

# PUZZLE #4

| | | |
|---|---|---|
| Asteroid | Meteor | Solar System |
| Comet | Orbit | Star |
| Constellation | Planet | Sun |
| Cosmos | Pluto | Universe |
| Earth | Rocket | Uranus |
| Mars | Saturn | Venus |

# PUZZLE #5

| | | |
|---|---|---|
| Agriculture | Egg | Pail |
| Animals | Gate | Scarecrow |
| Calf | Goat | Sheep |
| Coop | Haystack | Silo |
| Corn | Hen | Swine |
| Cow | Hog | Tiller |
| Dairy | Horse | Tractor |
| Dog | Lamb | |

# PUZZLE #6

| Aardvark | Hippo | Monkey |
| Antelope | Hyena | Nyala |
| Baboon | Impala | Porcupine |
| Buffalo | Jackal | Zebra |
| Duiker | Kudu | |
| Giraffe | Lion | |

# PUZZLE #7

| Algae | Current | Manta Ray | Salmon |
|-------|---------|-----------|--------|
| Anemone | Eel | Ocean | Shark |
| Barnacle | Flounder | Otter | Tide |
| Clam | Kelp | Plankton | Turtle |
| Coral | Manatee | Reef | |

# PUZZLE #8

| Airplane | Elevator | Locomotive | Spaceship |
| Barge | Ferry | Raft | Taxi |
| Battleship | Glider | Rocket | Toboggan |
| Chopper | Jeep | Snowmobile | Tugboat |

# PUZZLE #9

| Acorn | Fall | Leaf | Rake |
| Apple | Feast | November | Squash |
| Chestnut | Football | October | Turkey |
| Cider | Hay Ride | Pumpkin | |

# PUZZLE #10

| Accordion | Gong | Maracas | Saxophone |
|-----------|------|---------|-----------|
| Banjo | Guitar | Oboe | Sitar |
| Bell | Harmonica | Organ | Trombone |
| Cello | Harp | Piccolo | |
| Drum | Lute | Recorder | |

# CRYPTOGRAMS

Cryptograms are simple-substitution ciphers in which every letter of the alphabet has been switched to another. Your task is to use pattern recognition and your grammar and vocabulary abilities to decipher the hidden quote.

Hint: start with the 1, 2, and 3 letter words, and remember that the most common letters in the English language are E-T-A-I-O-N, in roughly that order.

# PUZZLE #1

S̄R̄ N̄D̄W̄R̄ D̄ H̄ȲL̄ȲŪ T̄

K̄P̄ S̄X̄D̄V̄ S̄R̄ T̄R̄V̄,

K̄Ō V̄ S̄R̄ N̄D̄W̄R̄ D̄ H̄ȲĀ R̄

K̄P̄ S̄X̄D̄V̄ S̄R̄ T̄ȲL̄R̄.

Hint: The first four words of this quote are "We make a living".

# PUZZLE #2

P̄L̄Ā F̄L̄R̄ M̄ḠF̄ ḠP̄H̄ L̄R̄Q̄R̄J̄

Ō P̄S̄R̄ P̄ Ō T̄H̄D̄P̄E R̄ ḠP̄H̄

L̄R̄Q̄R̄J̄ D̄J̄T̄R̄S̄

P̄L̄Ā D̄ḠT̄L̄Ȳ L̄R̄M̄.

Hint: The seventh word is "mistake".

# PUZZLE #3

A̅J̅Q̅  T̅S̅M̅R̅  K̅T̅W̅Q̅

A̅J̅P̅S̅N̅  C̅O̅T̅T̅A̅  M̅T̅V̅X̅

P̅K̅  A̅J̅C̅A̅  P̅A̅  G̅P̅M̅M̅

V̅J̅C̅S̅N̅Q̅ .

Hint: The last word in the quote is "change".

# PUZZLE #4

O̅P̅A̅  D̅N̅O̅N̅T̅A̅  C̅A̅B̅Z̅S̅T̅R̅

O̅Z̅  O̅P̅Z̅R̅A̅  Y̅P̅Z̅

C̅A̅B̅V̅A̅X̅A̅  V̅S̅  O̅P̅A̅

C̅A̅G̅N̅O̅K̅  Z̅D̅  O̅P̅A̅V̅T̅

H̅T̅A̅G̅F̅R̅ .

Hint: The last three words are "of their dreams".

# PUZZLE #5

$$\overline{JCPCU} \quad \overline{OCXU} \quad \overline{FEXQMZF}.$$

$$\overline{GECT} \quad \overline{FKSHWT} \quad \overline{SCXJ}$$

$$\overline{GEXG} \quad \overline{GECUC} \cdot \overline{F} \quad \overline{X}$$

$$\overline{WKREG} \quad \overline{FMSCZECUC}$$

$$\overline{JCXUTT}.$$

Hint: The third word in the quote is "shadows".

# PUZZLE #6

$$\overline{RJB} \quad \overline{UGWQR} \quad \overline{QRBC}$$

$$\overline{RDNLWK} \quad \overline{TWBLROBQQ}$$

$$\overline{GQ} \quad \overline{RD} \quad \overline{AB} \quad \overline{JDOBQR}.$$

Hint: The last word in the quote is "honest".

# PUZZLE #7

$$\overline{Q\,P\,H} \quad \overline{A\,K\,Z\,Z} \quad \overline{J\,T\,W\,T\,B} \quad \overline{U\,P}$$

$$\overline{T\,J\,Q\,S\,C\,K\,J\,F} \quad \overline{K\,J} \quad \overline{S\,C\,K\,D}$$

$$\overline{A\,P\,B\,Z\,U} \quad \overline{A\,K\,S\,C\,P\,H\,S}$$

$$\overline{E\,P\,H\,B\,T\,F\,T}\,.$$

Hint: The last two words are "without courage".

# PUZZLE #8

$$\overline{C\,V\,H\,Z\,O} \quad \overline{H\,E} \quad \overline{N\,R\,T\,P} \quad \overline{H\,E}$$

$$\overline{M\,S\,R} \quad \overline{T\,H\,O} \quad \overline{B\,P\,Y\,C\,V} \quad \overline{M\,S\,R}$$

$$\overline{H\,Z\,V} \quad \overline{M\,S\,R\,O\,U}\,, \quad \overline{E\,Y\,O\,T\,V}$$

$$\overline{C\,Y\,T\,V} \quad \overline{L\,V\,T\,S\,N\,V} \quad \overline{W\,S\,S}$$

$$\overline{L\,R\,E\,M} \quad \overline{C\,H\,W\,V\,Z}\,.$$

Hint: The last two words are "busy later".

# PUZZLE #9

F JXTWU JFZ FLE

CRPLNTMZL NXFN F

GTLP VFZ JFZZMN

FZLGPK .

Hint: The last two words are "cannot answer".

# PUZZLE #10

XODTRVNBH'C TDLTBCX

NC VB LXTYRTX RH

XETVW ENHO ZNVA

RH BTXH BHX .

Hint: The fifth word is "replace".

# PUZZLE #11

L̅X̅W̅   U̅X̅Z̅'J̅   C̅V̅E̅K̅   J̅X̅

H̅K̅   Y̅O̅K̅V̅J̅   J̅X̅   M̅J̅V̅O̅J̅

H̅W̅J̅   L̅X̅W̅   C̅V̅E̅K̅   J̅X̅

M̅J̅V̅O̅J̅   J̅X̅   H̅K̅   Y̅O̅K̅V̅J̅ .

Hint: The first word is "you," and the last word is "great".

# PUZZLE #12

X̅B̅J̅   E̅V̅M̅   C̅V̅E̅W̅M̅V̅   L̅K̅E̅P̅

X̅B̅J̅   C̅M̅F̅S̅M̅W̅M̅ ,

Z̅L̅V̅B̅P̅R̅M̅V̅   L̅K̅E̅P̅   X̅B̅J̅

Z̅M̅M̅U̅   E̅P̅O̅   Z̅U̅E̅V̅L̅M̅V̅

L̅K̅E̅P̅   X̅B̅J̅   L̅K̅S̅P̅H̅ .

Hint: The last three words are "than you think".

# PUZZLE #13

P̄Q̄Q̄  Z̄T̄K̄X̄  C̄X̄H̄P̄W̄R̄  ḠP̄Ū

ḠT̄W̄H̄  V̄X̄K̄H̄  N̄B̄  Z̄T̄K̄

M̄P̄Ē H̄  V̄M̄H̄  ḠT̄K̄X̄P̄T̄H̄

V̄T̄  Ā K̄X̄R̄K̄H̄  V̄M̄H̄W̄.

Hint: The second and third words are "your dreams".

# PUZZLE #14

J̄K̄Z̄'P̄  D̄Ȳ Ū  T̄S̄D̄B̄H̄T̄S̄

L̄P̄'T̄  K̄N̄S̄Ȳ,  T̄V̄L̄F̄S̄

T̄S̄D̄B̄H̄T̄S̄  L̄P̄  X̄B̄ŌŌS̄Z̄S̄J̄.

Hint: The last two words are "it happened".

# PUZZLE #15

$\overline{BC}$ $\overline{BT}$ $\overline{JYCCYT}$ $\overline{CZ}$

$\overline{JY}$ $\overline{W}$ $\overline{AWBKQTY}$ $\overline{WC}$

$\overline{TZGYCXBME}$ $\overline{LZQ}$ $\overline{KZNY}$

$\overline{CXWM}$ $\overline{CZ}$ $\overline{JY}$ $\overline{W}$ $\overline{TQDDYTT}$

$\overline{WC}$ $\overline{TZGYCXBME}$ $\overline{LZQ}$ $\overline{XWCY}$.

Hint: The last three words are "something you hate".

# PUZZLE #16

$\overline{M}$ $\overline{VRDG}$ $\overline{GKS}$ $\overline{M}$ $\overline{GJL}$

$\overline{WKML}$ $\overline{XSTRMRO}$ $\overline{EBW}$

$\overline{M}$'$\overline{QD}$ $\overline{YKJRODC}$ $\overline{J}$ $\overline{ZDG}$

$\overline{WMXDL}$ $\overline{LMRYD}$ $\overline{WKDR}$.

Hint: The phrase "a few times" appears somewhere in this quote.

# PUZZLE #17

V̄Ē  R̄ĀP̄  B̄J̄ŌH̄  R̄ĀP̄Z̄

Ḡ Z̄ C̄ J̄ T̄ Q̄   H̄ Ā   F̄ Ā T̄ C̄

H̄ Z̄ P̄ C̄ ,   Ḡ Ā Ō ' H̄

Ā L̄ C̄ Z̄ Q̄ Ȳ C̄ C̄ Ū .

Hint: The last two words are "don't oversleep".

# PUZZLE #18

X̄  C̄S̄N̄N̄C̄J̄  Ḡ R̄ Ḡ Q̄ J̄ Ḡ Q̄ J̄

Ḡ R̄ Ō   X̄ Ḡ M̄   N̄ B̄ J̄ Ḡ ,

S̄ Q̄   T̄ B̄ J̄ U S̄ Q̄ B̄ J̄ M̄   K̄ W̄

N̄ B̄ J̄   Ō S̄ Q̄ J̄ Q̄ N̄   L̄ J̄ Ḡ .

Hint: The last two words are "wisest men".

# PUZZLE #19

$\overline{ET}$ $\overline{EA}$ $\overline{SFY}$ $\overline{KRSEKHA}$

$\overline{TRJT}$ $\overline{ARSV}$ $\overline{VRJT}$ $\overline{VH}$

$\overline{TYFDU}$ $\overline{JYH}$, $\overline{TJY}$ $\overline{GSYH}$

$\overline{TRJB}$ $\overline{SFY}$ $\overline{JWEDETEHA}$.

Hint: The last word is "abilities".

# PUZZLE #20

$\overline{QV}$ $\overline{TWVPT}$ $\overline{TS}$

$\overline{BFQPHYPT}$ $\overline{YL}$ $\overline{NTFHM}$ $\overline{Q}$

$\overline{BTWVO}$ $\overline{TS}$ $\overline{BFTQPMYVZ}$.

Hint: The last two words are "of preaching".

# DOT TO DOT

Start with the number 1, and draw a continuous line through each subsequent number (2, 3, 4, etc.) in order to reveal the hidden image!

# PUZZLE #1

**FUN FACT**

There are enough blood vessels in your body to circle the Earth ... twice!

# PUZZLE #2

**FUN FACT**

Pound for pound, lemons contain more sugar than strawberries.

# PUZZLE #3

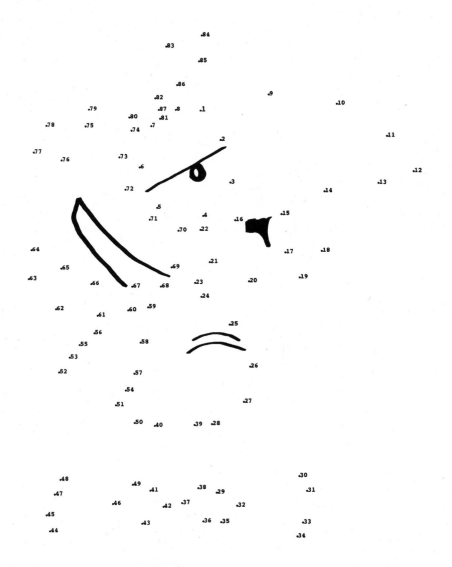

## Riddle

**WHAT GETS WETTER THE MORE IT DRIES?**

A towel

# PUZZLE #4

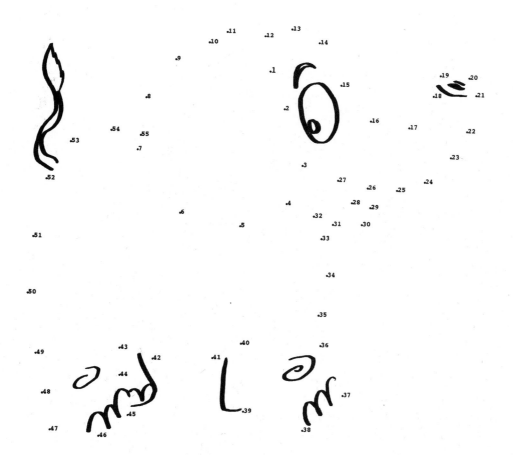

Riddle

**WHAT 5-LETTER WORD BECOMES ROUNDER WHEN YOU ADD TWO LETTERS TO IT?**

Round

# PUZZLE #5

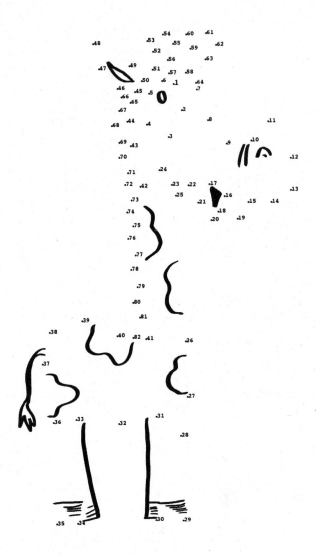

Giraffes have such long tongues that they can lick their own ears!

# PUZZLE #6

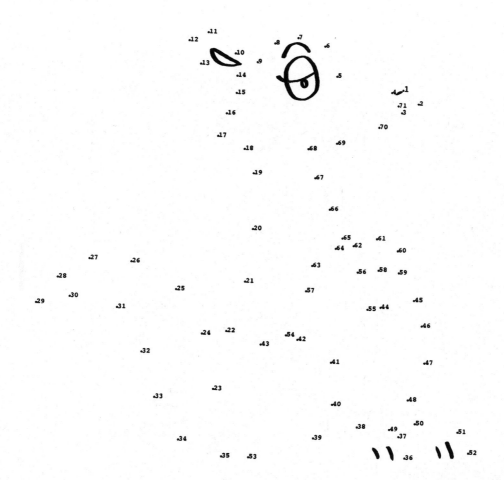

What do body builders and male kangaroos have in common? They both flex their biceps to impress females!

# PUZZLE #7

# PUZZLE #8

**FUN FACT**

Butterflies have taste sensors not in their mouths but on their feet!

# PUZZLE #9

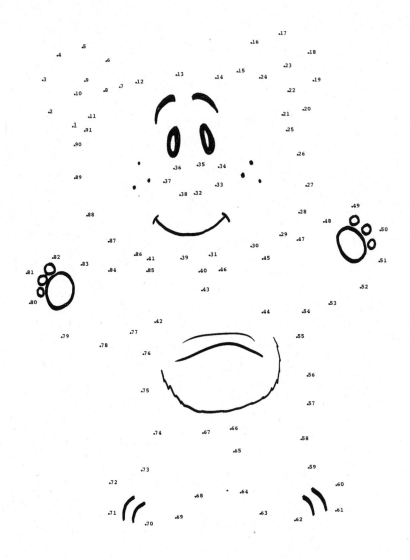

# PUZZLE #10

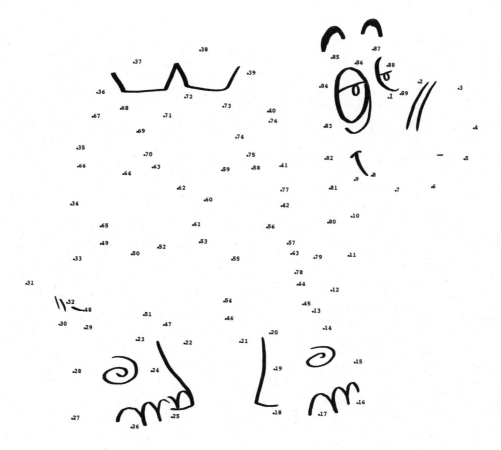

Add up all the coastline in the United States and you'll find that more than half of it is in Alaska alone!

# DROP QUOTES

Your goal with these puzzles is to uncover a hidden quote. A black-and-white crossword-style grid is set up for each quote, with a number of letters "hovering" above each column. Your task is to "drop" each of those letters into the appropriate square in each column, until the entire quote is revealed. All punctuation marks (commas, periods, dashes, etc.) have been removed, and some words may carry over from one row to the next.

# PUZZLE #1

Publilius Syrus

| | E | | C | E | | | | | | | | | | | |
| N | O | | O | R | I | E | K | D | O | | S | | T | H | L |
| H | H | E | T | N | A | N | S | N | O | W | U | N | W | I | A | T |

Hint: The word "until" appears in this puzzle.

# PUZZLE #2

Proverb

| | O | | R | R | | N | E | | | | | | |
| T | S | E | H | E | E | S | S | R | I | S | | T | W | A |
| Y | H | T | G | G | R | A | S | I | D | E | O | N | A | L | H | E |

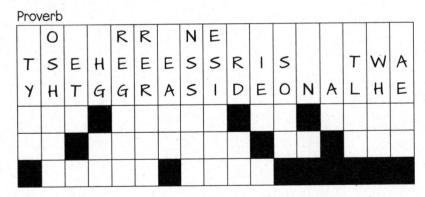

Hint: The word "grass" appears in this puzzle.

# PUZZLE #3

J.K. Rowling

| N |   |   | L | A |   |   | C |   |   |   | M | S | Y |   |
|---|---|---|---|---|---|---|---|---|---|---|---|---|---|---|
| W | E |   | W | A | T |   | M | S | S |   | I | G | A | T |
| N | H | E | H | H | L | T | I | I | S | R | B | E | H | K | E | E |
| T | D | W | A | C | H | O | I | U | E | T | E | A | T | W | E | A |

Hint: The words "choice" and "right" both appear in this puzzle.

# PUZZLE #4

Henry Ford

|   | Y |   | Y | K |   | Y | U |   | O |   |
|---|---|---|---|---|---|---|---|---|---|---|
| I | T | H | T | U | O | E | Y | O | A | N | O | T | R |
| W | H | K | O | N | R | R | R | I | G | H | T | T | H |
| T | N | E | I | H | E | U | Y | C | O | U | C | A | N |

Hint: The first word of this quote is "whether".

# PUZZLE #5

Lewis Carroll

| I | O | S |   |   |   |   |   |   |   |   |   |   |   |   |
|---|---|---|---|---|---|---|---|---|---|---|---|---|---|---|
| S | N | M | E |   |   | E | E |   | I |   | Y |   | A |   |
| F | E | V | T | D | M | M | O | S | R | A | V | E | A | S | K |
| I | I | X | E | I | I | P | F | S | M | E | B | L | R | E | E | L |
| S | A | G | S | T | B | A | S | O | S | I | N | B | E | B | T | H |

Hint: The words "impossible" and "breakfast" both appear in this quote.

# PUZZLE #6

John Hays Hammond

| S |   | A | L |   |   | O |   |   |   |   |   |   |   |   |
|---|---|---|---|---|---|---|---|---|---|---|---|---|---|---|
| R | U | A | R | E | C | S | E | N |   | H | S |   | O | N |
| F | E | C | L | A | S | W | O | R | T | A | W | I | I | H | E |
| C | H | A | C | L | F | T | U | R | D | I | T | H | T | L | E | O |

Hint: The word "character" appears in this puzzle.

# PUZZLE #7

Proverb

| | | | | | | | | | | | | | | | | |
|---|---|---|---|---|---|---|---|---|---|---|---|---|---|---|---|---|
| T | | | N | | | G | O | | T | H | | | | | | |
| H | H | G | E | O | T | G | E | | G | O | I | | G | | G | E |
| W | S | E | T | T | U | H | H | I | N | G | E | N | T | O | U | G |
| | | | | ■ | | | | ■ | | | | | | ■ | | |
| | | ■ | | | | | | ■ | | | | ■ | | | | |
| | ■ | | | | ■ | | | | | | ■ | ■ | ■ | ■ | ■ | ■ |

Hint: The first letter in this quote is "W".

# PUZZLE #8

Aesop

| | | | | | | | | | | | | | |
|---|---|---|---|---|---|---|---|---|---|---|---|---|---|
| | E | | W | | S | | | M | | | | | |
| N | H | E | R | | T | M | A | F | E | D | T | E | |
| E | O | S | S | | W | O | O | L | L | T | I | S | R |
| N | V | O | A | C | N | A | S | T | A | K | I | N | D |
| | | ■ | | | | ■ | | | ■ | | | | |
| | | | | ■ | | | ■ | | | | | | |
| ■ | | | | ■ | | | | | | ■ | | | ■ |
| | | | | ■ | | | | | | | ■ | ■ | ■ |

Hint: The word "kindness" appears somewhere in this puzzle.

Walt Disney

```
H U . . R R S . . . . . . . . . .
O E L . R E N S . R . C . . N R . C
H A L D G N D A U O S E . . N R A C U
R I R M I E E O T E F T O U S T . T .
```

Hint: The words "greatest" and "resource" both appear in this puzzle.

# PUZZLE #10

Dr. Seuss

```
. . Y . . . . U . S . . . . E .
W L . T E N . D T . . A T . E N D
B E R T E O D H S H . A T E U I A O
D E O A H I R Y T E O Y H E . W F T
E H S B M C A U A O O N M S A . H N
T M A W A N W D O D N T R O M . H N
```

Hint: This quote begins: "Be who you are and say what you feel..."

# ELIMINATION QUOTES

We'll give you a series of letters for each of these puzzles, and your task is to "eliminate" each of them by filling them in with your pen or pencil. If you do it right, the letters that remain will spell out a hidden quote.

# PUZZLE #1

## ELIMINATION QUOTES

Color in all instances of these five letters (H, J, L, V, and X), and the letters that remain will spell out a hidden quote by Walt Disney.

## ELIMINATION QUOTES

Color in all instances of these five letters (C, D, J, P, and S), and the letters that remain will spell out a hidden quote by Oscar Wilde.

# P I J S A M P N S
# O J D T S Y S O U
# N S G E C N C O P
# U J D G D H T O K
# P N S O W D E J
# V E J D R D Y J T
# D D H I S N J G C

# PUZZLE #3

## ELIMINATION QUOTES

Color in all instances of these five letters (B, D, F, V, and Z), and the letters that remain will spell out a hidden quote by Sophocles.

F T H B E Z T V R U B T

B V H Z I D S F A B L W

F A Z Y D V S D T V H

D E Z S F T B R O F N B

G F Z E B S F T A R D G

B Z U M D E F N D T B

# PUZZLE #4

## ELIMINATION QUOTES

Color in all instances of these five letters (B, F, G, K, and V), and the letters that remain will spell out a hidden quote by Kenneth Branaugh.

F A D V U L K F T F K S G

A F B R G E K J U F G S B

T F V C V H I G L B D R E

K N G W H G B O E F A F

R N G M G O N F B E K Y

# PUZZLE #5

## ELIMINATION QUOTES

Color in all instances of these five letters (B, O, P, U, and W), and the letters that remain will spell out a hidden quote by Dr. Seuss.

F W A U P N B T A B S W

Y O I B S A U N E B C B E

W S P S U A O W R Y W I

N P G P O R W E D W I P

E W N U O T P I N O L U B

I B V O B I W P N O G B W

# LOGIC PUZZLES

Logic puzzles (also known as "logic grid puzzles") require you to use logic and reasoning to deduce the relationships among different people, places, or things based on a limited number of clues. Using only the clues provided, you must fill in the grid with X's (false relationships) and O's (true relationships) to determine the unique solution.

Always keep in mind that each item in the puzzle belongs to one and only one set. No item is ever paired with more than one item in each group.

# PUZZLE #1

## THROWING DARTS

The Palmerton County Darts Association held a friendly darts tournament this week. Each contestant used a different colored set of darts, and they each finished with different scores. Using only the clues that follow, match each player to his score, and determine the color of his darts.

**1** Of Shaun and Matthew, one finished with 62 points and the other threw the red darts.

**2** Felix, who threw the violet darts, scored 7 points higher than the contestant who threw the black ones.

**3** Shaun finished with a score of 55 points.

|  | | Players | | | | Colors | | |
|---|---|---|---|---|---|---|---|---|
| Scores | Felix | Hubert | Matthew | Shaun | Black | Green | Red | Violet |
| 41 | | | | | | | | |
| 48 | | | | | | | | |
| 55 | | | | | | | | |
| 62 | | | | | | | | |
| Black | | | | | | | | |
| Green | | | | | | | | |
| Red | | | | | | | | |
| Violet | | | | | | | | |

| Scores | Players | Colors |
|---|---|---|
| 41 | | |
| 48 | | |
| 55 | | |
| 62 | | |

# PUZZLE #2

## ATHLETE OF THE YEAR

The Appleton High School yearbook committee held a vote today to determine who would be named "Athlete of the Year". Each of the four contestants play a different sport, and each received a different number of votes. Using only the clues below, determine how many votes each student received, and what sport each of them plays.

**1** Of Colin and Ken, one plays soccer and the other received 18 votes.

**2** The basketball player received 7 fewer votes than the soccer star.

**3** Tommy received 25 votes.

**4** Colin plays football.

| | | Contestants | | | | Sports | | | |
|---|---|---|---|---|---|---|---|---|---|
| | | Colin | Ken | Pablo | Tommy | Basketball | Football | Hockey | Soccer |
| Votes | 4 | | | | | | | | |
| | 11 | | | | | | | | |
| | 18 | | | | | | | | |
| | 25 | | | | | | | | |
| Sports | Basketball | | | | | | | | |
| | Football | | | | | | | | |
| | Hockey | | | | | | | | |
| | Soccer | | | | | | | | |

| Votes | Contestants | Sports |
|---|---|---|
| 4 | | |
| 11 | | |
| 18 | | |
| 25 | | |

# PUZZLE #3

## THE FUN RUN

Coalinga County's annual "Fun Run" was held this weekend. Each of the top four runners wore a different colored shirt and had a different finishing time. Using only the clues that follow, match each of the runners to his shirt color and determine each of their final run times.

**1** Ralph didn't finish in 22 minutes.

**2** Of the two runners in the red and black shirts, one finished in 24 minutes and the other was Ralph.

**3** Of Patrick and Daryl, one wore the silver shirt and the other finished in 24 minutes.

**4** The runner wearing the red shirt finished 3 minutes after Anthony.

**5** Of Patrick and the runner in the pink shirt, one finished in 21 minutes and the other completed the race in 25 minutes.

**6** Daryl is very superstitious—he has never worn a black shirt while racing.

|  | | Anthony | Daryl | Orlando | Patrick | Ralph | Black | Orange | Pink | Red | Silver |
|---|---|---|---|---|---|---|---|---|---|---|---|
| **Times** | 21 minutes | | | | | | | | | | |
| | 22 minutes | | | | | | | | | | |
| | 23 minutes | | | | | | | | | | |
| | 24 minutes | | | | | | | | | | |
| | 25 minutes | | | | | | | | | | |
| **Shirt Colors** | Black | | | | | | | | | | |
| | Orange | | | | | | | | | | |
| | Pink | | | | | | | | | | |
| | Red | | | | | | | | | | |
| | Silver | | | | | | | | | | |

| Times | Runners | Shirt Colors |
|---|---|---|
| 21 minutes | | |
| 22 minutes | | |
| 23 minutes | | |
| 24 minutes | | |
| 25 minutes | | |

# PUZZLE #4

## PETE'S PET STORE

Pete runs a pet store in downtown Finnerton. In the past several months, he's sold five different birds, each in a different month and each sold by a different salesperson. Using only the clues below, determine who sold each bird, and figure out the month in which each sale took place.

1  The canary was sold one month before Pam made her sale.

2  Pam sold her bird in either January or March.

3  Sara sold her bird in February.

4  Of the two birds sold by Pam and Olivia, one was sold in January and the other was the lovebird.

5  The bird sold in April is either the parrot or the lovebird.

6  The canary was bought sometime after the macaw.

7  Velma didn't work at the pet store at all in the month of May.

|  | | Ida | Olivia | Pam | Sara | Velma | Canary | Lorikeet | Lovebird | Macaw | Parrot |
|---|---|---|---|---|---|---|---|---|---|---|---|
| **Months** | January | | | | | | | | | | |
| | February | | | | | | | | | | |
| | March | | | | | | | | | | |
| | April | | | | | | | | | | |
| | May | | | | | | | | | | |
| **Birds** | Canary | | | | | | | | | | |
| | Lorikeet | | | | | | | | | | |
| | Lovebird | | | | | | | | | | |
| | Macaw | | | | | | | | | | |
| | Parrot | | | | | | | | | | |

| Months | Names | Birds |
|---|---|---|
| January | | |
| February | | |
| March | | |
| April | | |
| May | | |

# PUZZLE #5

## THE WORLD'S RICHEST PEOPLE

Sandra is writing an article about some of the world's richest people. She's selected five different people to feature in her piece. Each of them lives in a different country, and each has a different total net worth (in dollars). Using only the clues that follow, determine the home country and net worth of each of Sandra's five subjects.

**1** The person living in France is worth 2 billion less than Betty Bush, who doesn't live in Sweden.

**2** Nadine Newton lives in Hamburg, Germany.

**3** The person with the most money is either the one from Argentina or Faith Flynn.

**4** Gil Gallegos, who is worth $28 billion, has somewhat less money than Tim Townsend.

|  | | Betty Bush | Faith Flynn | Gil Gallegos | Nadine Newton | Tim Townsend | Argentina | England | France | Germany | Sweden |
|---|---|---|---|---|---|---|---|---|---|---|---|
| **Wealth** | $25 Billion | | | | | | | | | | |
| | $26 Billion | | | | | | | | | | |
| | $27 Billion | | | | | | | | | | |
| | $28 Billion | | | | | | | | | | |
| | $29 Billion | | | | | | | | | | |
| **Countries** | Argentina | | | | | | | | | | |
| | England | | | | | | | | | | |
| | France | | | | | | | | | | |
| | Germany | | | | | | | | | | |
| | Sweden | | | | | | | | | | |

| Wealth | People | Countries |
|---|---|---|
| $25 Billion | | |
| $26 Billion | | |
| $27 Billion | | |
| $28 Billion | | |
| $29 Billion | | |

# PUZZLE #6

## SALON APPOINTMENTS

Sal's Salon has a full schedule today! There are five customers coming in today, each at a different time and each scheduled with a different stylist. Using only the clues below, match each customer to her stylist and appointment time.

**1** Myra's appointment is at 11:00am.

**2** Cristina doesn't have the 3:00pm appointment.

**3** Alison will come in 3 hours before Rhonda's client.

**4** Pam's client has her appointment one hour *before* Alison's.

**5** Susie's customer will come in sometime after Nettie's.

**6** Blanche only ever gets her hair done by Yvonne. She has the 2:00pm appointment.

|  |  | Alison | Blanche | Cristina | Dolores | Myra | Nettie | Pam | Rhonda | Susie | Yvonne |
|---|---|---|---|---|---|---|---|---|---|---|---|
| | 11:00am | | | | | | | | | | |
| | 12:00pm | | | | | | | | | | |
| | 1:00pm | | | | | | | | | | |
| | 2:00pm | | | | | | | | | | |
| | 3:00pm | | | | | | | | | | |
| | Nettie | | | | | | | | | | |
| | Pam | | | | | | | | | | |
| | Rhonda | | | | | | | | | | |
| | Susie | | | | | | | | | | |
| | Yvonne | | | | | | | | | | |

| Times | Customers | Stylists |
|---|---|---|
| 11:00am | | |
| 12:00pm | | |
| 1:00pm | | |
| 2:00pm | | |
| 3:00pm | | |

# PUZZLE #7

## BEST IN SHOW

The Bennington Kennel Club is putting together a feature article on some of their past dog show winners. Each of the five dogs featured has a different owner and is a different breed, and each won "Best in Show" in a different year. Using only the clues below, match each dog to its breed and owner, and determine the year in which it won "Best in Show".

1  Of Ginger's dog and Douglas's dog, one is the dalmatian and the other won in 2008.

2  Of the dogs that won in 2007 and 2010, one is the chow chow and the other is Elsie's.

3  The chow chow won 1 year after Barbara's dog.

4  Either the Irish setter or the beagle won in 2008.

5  Fernando's dog won sometime after the beagle.

6  Ginger's dog won in 2009.

|  | Owners | | | | | Breeds | | | | |
|---|---|---|---|---|---|---|---|---|---|---|
|  | Barbara | Douglas | Elsie | Fernando | Ginger | Beagle | Chow Chow | Dalmatian | Great Dane | Irish Setter |
| 2006 | | | | | | | | | | |
| 2007 | | | | | | | | | | |
| 2008 | | | | | | | | | | |
| 2009 | | | | | | | | | | |
| 2010 | | | | | | | | | | |
| Beagle | | | | | | | | | | |
| Chow Chow | | | | | | | | | | |
| Dalmatian | | | | | | | | | | |
| Great Dane | | | | | | | | | | |
| Irish Setter | | | | | | | | | | |

| Years | Owners | Breeds |
|---|---|---|
| 2006 | | |
| 2007 | | |
| 2008 | | |
| 2009 | | |
| 2010 | | |

# PUZZLE #8

## PAM'S PARTY SHOP

Pam runs "Parties Unlimited"—a shop that caters to a wide variety of special party-related requests (such as clowns or magicians) for its clients. She has four different jobs scheduled for this week, each on a different day, and each involving a different request from a different family. Using only the clues below, match each of this week's bookings with its date, family, and special request, and determine the location of each.

1 The Ingrams' party on Terrace Avenue will be on October 3.

2 The Thornton family event is either the one on October 6 or the one that rented the photo booth.

3 The booking on Island Drive is 2 days after the Garner family event.

4 Of the two bookings by the Ingrams and the Thorntons, one is on Holly Street and the other requested a rock band.

5 The magician will go either to Ronald Street or to the Ingrams' party.

| | | Requests | | | | Families | | | | Locations | | | |
|---|---|---|---|---|---|---|---|---|---|---|---|---|---|
| | | Bounce Castle | Magician | Photo Booth | Rock Band | Garner | Ingram | O'Connor | Thornton | Holly Street | Island Drive | Ronald Street | Terrace Avenue |
| Days | October 3 | | | | | | | | | | | | |
| | October 4 | | | | | | | | | | | | |
| | October 5 | | | | | | | | | | | | |
| | October 6 | | | | | | | | | | | | |
| Locations | Holly Street | | | | | | | | | | | | |
| | Island Drive | | | | | | | | | | | | |
| | Ronald Street | | | | | | | | | | | | |
| | Terrace Avenue | | | | | | | | | | | | |
| Families | Garner | | | | | | | | | | | | |
| | Ingram | | | | | | | | | | | | |
| | O'Connor | | | | | | | | | | | | |
| | Thornton | | | | | | | | | | | | |

| Days | Requests | Families | Locations |
|---|---|---|---|
| October 3 | | | |
| October 4 | | | |
| October 5 | | | |
| October 6 | | | |

# PUZZLE #9

## INTERNATIONAL DIPLOMACY

The State Department is sending out four of its diplomats on different missions over the next several months. Each diplomat will go to a different capital city, and each trip will last a different number of days. No two diplomats will depart in the same month. Using only the clues that follow, determine the destination and duration of each diplomats trip, as well as the month in which each will depart.

**1** Whoever is going to Paris will leave sometime before Nancy Nguyen, who will leave 2 months before the diplomat with the 7 day visit.

**2** Umberto Underwood, who will depart sometime after Peter Pickett, is either the diplomat leaving in February or the one with the 4 day trip.

**3** The 6-day trip doesn't begin in February.

**4** The Warsaw mission will last for 7 days.

**5** Of Edna Ellison and the diplomat leaving in February, one is going to Warsaw and the other to Lisbon.

|  | | Diplomats | | | | Durations | | | | Capitals | | | |
|---|---|---|---|---|---|---|---|---|---|---|---|---|---|
|  | | Ellison | Nguyen | Pickett | Underwood | 4 Days | 6 Days | 7 Days | 9 Days | Kiev | Lisbon | Paris | Warsaw |
| **Months** | January | | | | | | | | | | | | |
| | February | | | | | | | | | | | | |
| | March | | | | | | | | | | | | |
| | April | | | | | | | | | | | | |
| **Capitals** | Kiev | | | | | | | | | | | | |
| | Lisbon | | | | | | | | | | | | |
| | Paris | | | | | | | | | | | | |
| | Warsaw | | | | | | | | | | | | |
| **Durations** | 4 Days | | | | | | | | | | | | |
| | 6 Days | | | | | | | | | | | | |
| | 7 Days | | | | | | | | | | | | |
| | 9 Days | | | | | | | | | | | | |

| Months | Diplomats | Durations | Capitals |
|---|---|---|---|
| January | | | |
| February | | | |
| March | | | |
| April | | | |

# PUZZLE #10

## LOTTERY WINNERS

This week's national lottery ended up with four different winners! Each lives in a different state and has a different occupation, and none of the four won the same amount of money. Using only the clues below, match each winner to his or her home state and occupation, and determine the total prize money won by each.

1  Cal Chandler won 5 million dollars less than Ed Elliott.

2  Of the teacher and the person from Georgia, one won $15 million and the other $5 million.

3  The $5 million winner was either the judge or the Iowan.

4  The lawyer, the person who won $15 million, and Betty Baxter are three different people.

5  The banker won less than $20 million.

6  The Hawaiian won less money than Betty Baxter, but it was still $5 million more than what the teacher won.

7  Either Betty Baxter or Hilda Hunt is from Georgia.

|  | | | Winners | | | | States | | | | Occupations | | | |
|---|---|---|---|---|---|---|---|---|---|---|---|---|---|---|
|  | | Betty Baxter | Cal Chandler | Ed Elliott | Hilda Hunt | Florida | Georgia | Hawaii | Iowa | Banker | Judge | Lawyer | Teacher |
| Winnings | $5 Million | | | | | | | | | | | | |
| | $10 Million | | | | | | | | | | | | |
| | $15 Million | | | | | | | | | | | | |
| | $20 Million | | | | | | | | | | | | |
| Occupations | Banker | | | | | | | | | | | | |
| | Judge | | | | | | | | | | | | |
| | Lawyer | | | | | | | | | | | | |
| | Teacher | | | | | | | | | | | | |
| States | Florida | | | | | | | | | | | | |
| | Georgia | | | | | | | | | | | | |
| | Hawaii | | | | | | | | | | | | |
| | Iowa | | | | | | | | | | | | |

| Winnings | Winners | States | Occupations |
|---|---|---|---|
| $5 Million | | | |
| $10 Million | | | |
| $15 Million | | | |
| $20 Million | | | |

# MATHDOKU

Mathdoku puzzles are a mix between math puzzles and sudoku puzzles. You're given a partially filled-in grid, and you must enter the numbers 1 through 9 into each empty white square, using each number exactly once, so that all six mathematical equations on the grid are fulfilled.

Each puzzle has one and only one unique solution, and all puzzles can be solved using only pure logical deduction.

# PUZZLE #1

| | × | | + | | = | 17 |
|---|---|---|---|---|---|---|
| × | | × | | × | | |
| 6 | × | | − | 2 | = | 16 |
| − | | + | | − | | |
| | + | 5 | + | | = | 16 |
| = | | = | | = | | |
| 47 | | 8 | | 12 | | |

# PUZZLE #2

| | × | 7 | − | | = | 34 |
|---|---|---|---|---|---|---|
| ÷ | | × | | + | | |
| | − | | + | 3 | = | 2 |
| + | | + | | + | | |
| | + | | + | 5 | = | 18 |
| = | | = | | = | | |
| 15 | | 18 | | 16 | | |

# PUZZLE #3

| | + | | + | | = | 13 |
|---|---|---|---|---|---|---|
| + | | − | | × | | |
| | × | | − | | = | 13 |
| + | | + | | + | | |
| 6 | − | 1 | + | 9 | = | 14 |
| = | | = | | = | | |
| 13 | | 0 | | 65 | | |

# PUZZLE #4

| | ÷ | | + | 2 | = | 4 |
|---|---|---|---|---|---|---|
| + | | + | | + | | |
| | + | 9 | + | | = | 24 |
| + | | − | | + | | |
| 5 | + | | − | | = | 2 |
| = | | = | | = | | |
| 18 | | 11 | | 14 | | |

# PUZZLE #5

| 7 | ÷ |   | + |   | = | 12 |
|---|---|---|---|---|---|----|
| × |   | − |   | + |   |    |
|   | + | 2 | − |   | = | 1  |
| + |   | + |   | + |   |    |
|   | × |   | + | 6 | = | 78 |
| = |   | = |   | = |   |    |
| 30 |  | 7 |   | 15 |  |    |

# PUZZLE #6

|   | − |   | + | 6 | = | 8  |
|---|---|---|---|---|---|----|
| + |   | + |   | × |   |    |
| 9 | × |   | + |   | = | 71 |
| − |   | + |   | + |   |    |
|   | + |   | + |   | = | 7  |
| = |   | = |   | = |   |    |
| 12 |  | 14 |  | 49 |  |    |

# PUZZLE #7

|   | × |   | + | 2 | = | 29 |
|---|---|---|---|---|---|----|
| × |   | + |   | × |   |    |
|   | + | 5 | + |   | = | 18 |
| + |   | − |   | + |   |    |
|   | × |   | + |   | = | 12 |
| = |   | = |   | = |   |    |
| 64 |  | 0 |   | 16 |  |    |

# PUZZLE #8

|   | × |   | + | 7 | = | 43 |
|---|---|---|---|---|---|----|
| + |   | ÷ |   | + |   |    |
| 6 | ÷ |   | − |   | = | 0  |
| − |   | + |   | − |   |    |
|   | − |   | + |   | = | 12 |
| = |   | = |   | = |   |    |
| 10 |  | 3 |   | 2 |  |    |

# PUZZLE #9

| | × | | + | | = | 12 |
|---|---|---|---|---|---|---|
| × | | × | | + | | |
| | − | 4 | + | | = | 10 |
| + | | + | | + | | |
| | × | | − | | = | 9 |
| = | | = | | = | | |
| 56 | | 11 | | 16 | | |

# PUZZLE #10

| | × | 3 | + | | = | 35 |
|---|---|---|---|---|---|---|
| ÷ | | + | | + | | |
| | × | | + | | = | 7 |
| + | | − | | + | | |
| | × | | − | | = | 22 |
| = | | = | | = | | |
| 16 | | 1 | | 19 | | |

# MAZES

Can you find your way out of each of these brain-bending mazes? Start by placing your pencil at the "START" point, and see if you can find your way around the maze all the way to the "FINISH"!

# PUZZLE #2

# PUZZLE #3

# PUZZLE #4

# PUZZLE #6

# PUZZLE #7

# PUZZLE #8

# PUZZLE #10

# MORE OR LESS

**(4X4)**

In these puzzles your task is to uncover the unique solution in which all "greater than" equations are satisfied, using only the numbers 1 through 4.

Each number is used once, and only once, in each row and column. And each pair of numbers that has a "greater than" sign between them must adhere to that requirement. Every puzzle has only one solution, and each solution can be reached using pure logic alone.

Note: Unlike in the Neighbor puzzles, here the absence of a "greater than" sign between any two numbers signifies nothing. It does not preclude one number from being greater than the other.

# PUZZLE #1

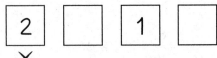

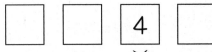
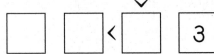
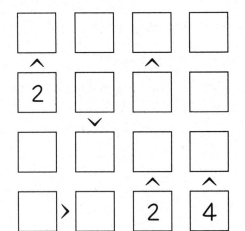

# PUZZLE #2

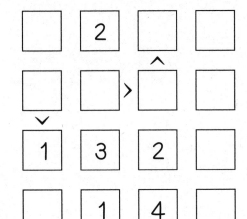
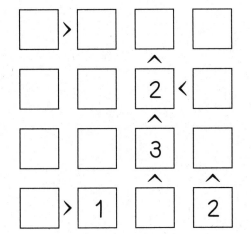

# PUZZLE #3

# PUZZLE #4

# PUZZLE #5

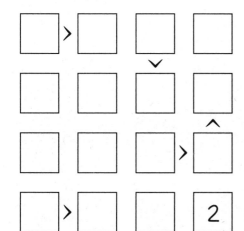

# PUZZLE #6

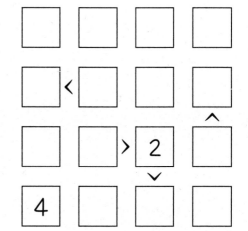

# PUZZLE #7

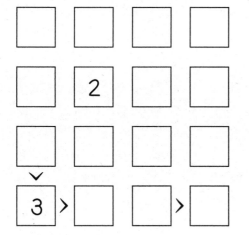

# PUZZLE #8

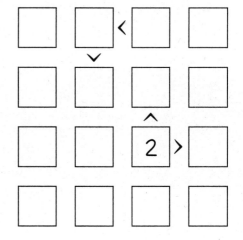

# MORE OR LESS

## (5X5)

These puzzles follow exactly the same rules as the 4x4 More or Less puzzles, except these require you to use the numbers 1 through 5. They're a bit larger, and a bit more difficult, but all the same rules apply. Good luck!

# PUZZLE #1

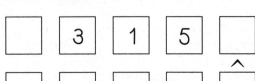
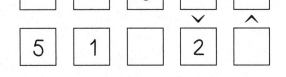

# PUZZLE #2

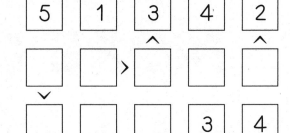
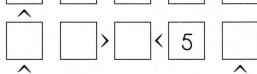

# PUZZLE #3

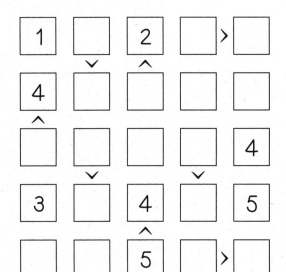

# PUZZLE #4

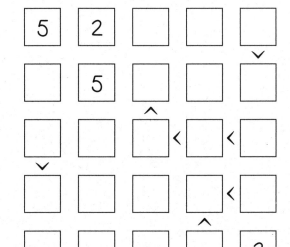

# PUZZLE #5

# PUZZLE #6

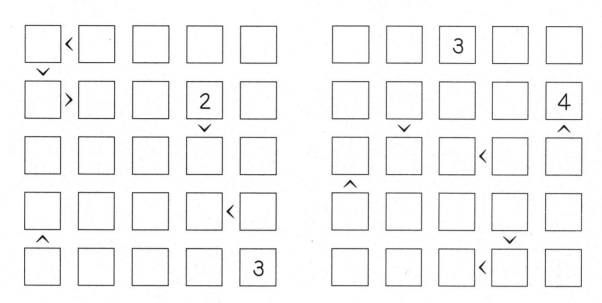

# MORSE CODE

Morse code was developed in the 19<sup>th</sup> century to help transmit messages via the newly-invented telegraph. Each letter in the alphabet is represented by a unique series of dots and dashes. Using the key below, see if you can decode the answers to the following jokes!

| A | B | C | D | E | F | G |
|---|---|---|---|---|---|---|
| ·— | —··· | —·—· | —·· | · | ··—· | ——· |

| H | I | J | K | L | M | N |
|---|---|---|---|---|---|---|
| ···· | ·· | ·——— | —·— | ·—·· | —— | —· |

| O | P | Q | R | S | T | U |
|---|---|---|---|---|---|---|
| ——— | ·——· | ——·— | ·—· | ··· | — | ··— |

| V | W | X | Y | Z |
|---|---|---|---|---|
| ···— | ·—— | —··— | —·—— | ——·· |

# PUZZLE #1
## WHAT DO TREES DRINK?

.-- --- --- -

-... . - .--

# PUZZLE #2
## DID YOU HEAR 19 AND 20 GOT INTO A FIGHT?

- .-- . -.. - -...

.-- --- -.

# PUZZLE #3
## HOW DOES THE OCEAN SAY HELLO?

.. - .-- .- ...- . ...

# PUZZLE #4
## WHAT'S THE BRIGHTEST ANIMAL IN THE SEA?

.-

... - .- .-. ...-. .. ... ....

# PUZZLE #5

## WHAT DO TWO PORCUPINES SAY WHEN THEY KISS?

--- ··- -··- ····

# PUZZLE #6

## WHAT DID ONE PLATE SAY TO THE OTHER?

-·· ·· -·· -·· · ·--

·· ··· --- -·· -- ·

# PUZZLE #7

## WHAT KIND OF CAR DID MICKEY MOUSE BUY FOR HIS WIFE?

·-

-- ·· -·· -·· ·· ·

···· ·· -·

# PUZZLE #8

## WHO MAKES THEIR LIVING BY DRIVING THEIR CUSTOMERS AWAY?

# PUZZLE #9

## HOW DO YOU OPEN A LOCKED BANANA?

# PUZZLE #10

## WHAT DO YOU CALL AN ALLIGATOR DETECTIVE?

# NEIGHBORS
### (4X4)

In these puzzles your task is to uncover the unique solution in which all "neighbor" requirements are satisfied, using only the numbers 1 through 4.

Each number is used once, and only once, in each row and column. And each pair of numbers that has a *black bar* between them must be "neighbors" on the number line: meaning one number is either 1 digit higher or 1 digit lower than the other. For example, the neighbors of 3 would be 2 and 4. The neighbors of 5 would be 4 and 6. 1 has only one neighbor (2), and 4 has only one neighbor (3).

Every puzzle has only one solution, and each solution can be reached using pure logic alone.

Remember: The absence of a "neighbor bar" between any two numbers is significant! It means those two numbers are definitely *not* neighbors. Be sure to keep this in mind!

# PUZZLE #1

|     | 4 |     | 1 |
|-----|---|-----|---|
| 2   |   |     | 4 |
| 4   |   |     | 2 |
| 1   |   |     |   |

# PUZZLE #2

| 3   |   |     | 2 |
|-----|---|-----|---|
|     |   |     | 4 |
| 2   |   | 3   | 1 |
| 4   |   |     |   |

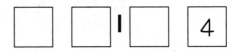

# PUZZLE #3

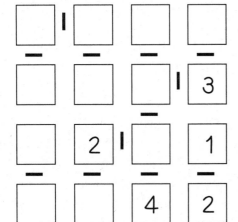

|     |   |     |   |
|-----|---|-----|---|
|     |   |     | 3 |
|     | 2 |     | 1 |
|     |   | 4   | 2 |

# PUZZLE #4

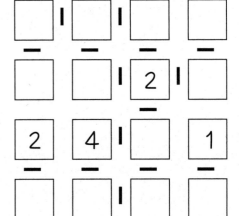

|     |   |     |   |
|-----|---|-----|---|
|     |   | 2   |   |
| 2   | 4 |     | 1 |
|     |   |     |   |

## PUZZLE #5

| | | | |
|---|---|---|---|
| 4 | | | |
| | 1 | | |
| | | | |
| 2 | | 1 | 3 |

## PUZZLE #6

| | | | |
|---|---|---|---|
| | | | |
| | | | |
| 3 | | | |
| | | | 4 |

## PUZZLE #7

| | | | |
|---|---|---|---|
| | | | |
| | | | |
| | | 1 | |
| | | | |

## PUZZLE #8

| | | | |
|---|---|---|---|
| | | | |
| | | 4 | |
| | | | |
| | | | |

# NEIGHBORS
## (5X5)

These puzzles follow exactly the same rules as the 4x4 Neighbor puzzles, except these require you to use the numbers 1 through 5. They're a bit larger, and a bit more difficult, but all the same rules apply. Good luck!

# PUZZLE #1

| 2 | 3 |   | 5 |   |
|---|---|---|---|---|
|   | 4 | 1 |   |   |
| 3 |   | 5 |   |   |
|   | 5 |   |   |   |
| 4 |   | 2 | 3 | 5 |

# PUZZLE #2

| 3 | 4 |   |   | 1 |
|---|---|---|---|---|
|   |   |   |   | 5 |
|   |   | 5 |   | 3 |
|   |   |   | 1 | 4 |
|   |   |   | 4 |   |

# PUZZLE #3

|   |   | 3 |   |   |
|---|---|---|---|---|
| 4 |   |   |   |   |
|   |   |   |   |   |
|   | 4 | 5 |   | 1 |
|   |   | 4 |   |   |

# PUZZLE #4

| 5 |   |   |   |   |
|---|---|---|---|---|
|   | 3 |   | 5 |   |
| 2 |   |   | 3 |   |
|   |   |   | 1 | 2 |
| 1 |   |   |   |   |

# PUZZLE #5

# PUZZLE #6

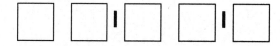

# PUZZLE #7

# PUZZLE #8

# PATHWAYS

In a Pathway puzzle, your goal is to draw lines connecting each pair of numbers to itself in such a way so that no lines ever cross. You can move horizontally and vertically across each box in the grid, but never diagonally. Every box in the grid must contain one line when the puzzle is completed. (The example below shows how it works.)

Be sure to use a pencil and eraser ... some of these can be quite tricky! Good luck!

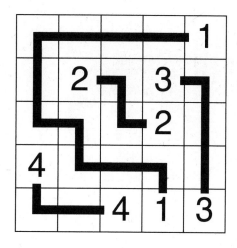

# PUZZLE #1

(4X4)

| 1 | 2 |   |   |
|---|---|---|---|
|   |   | 1 |   |
| 2 |   |   |   |
| 3 |   |   | 3 |

# PUZZLE #2

(4X4)

|   |   |   | 2 |
|---|---|---|---|
|   | 3 | 1 |   |
|   |   |   |   |
|   | 1 | 3 | 2 |

# PUZZLE #3

(5X5)

| | 1 | | | 2 |
|---|---|---|---|---|
| | | | | 3 |
| | 2 | 4 | | 5 |
| | | | 3 | |
| 1 | 4 | 5 | | |

# PUZZLE #4

(5X5)

| 1 | | | 1 | 2 |
|---|---|---|---|---|
| | | | | |
| | 3 | 4 | | 5 |
| | | | | |
| | 2 | 3 | 4 | 5 |

# PUZZLE #5

(5X5)

| 1 | | 2 | 3 | 4 |
|---|---|---|---|---|
| 2 | | | | |
| | 1 | | | |
| | | | 3 | |
| 4 | | | | |

# PUZZLE #6

(5X5)

| | | | | |
|---|---|---|---|---|
| | | | | |
| | | 3 | 2 | |
| | | 2 | 1 | |
| | | 1 | | 3 |

# PUZZLE #7

## (6X6)

| | | | | | |
|---|---|---|---|---|---|
| 1 | | | | | |
| 2 | | | | | |
| 3 | | 3 | | | 1 |
| | | 4 | | | 2 |
| | | | | | 5 |
| 4 | 5 | 6 | | | 6 |

### Riddle

**CAN YOU NAME FOUR DAYS THAT START WITH THE LETTER "T"?**

Tuesday, Thursday, today, and tomorrow

# PUZZLE #8

## (6X6)

| 1 |   | 2 |   |   | 3 |
|---|---|---|---|---|---|
| 2 |   | 1 |   |   | 4 |
|   |   |   |   |   |   |
| 5 | 6 |   |   |   |   |
|   |   | 5 |   |   | 4 |
| 6 |   |   |   |   | 3 |

**FUN FACT**

Deserts aren't always hot! The largest desert in the world is Antarctica, which has an average temperature of around -70°F.

# PUZZLE #9

## (6X6)

| 1 |   |   |   | 2 |   |
|---|---|---|---|---|---|
|   |   |   |   | 1 |   |
|   | 4 | 3 |   | 4 |   |
|   |   |   |   | 5 |   |
|   |   |   |   |   |   |
| 3 | 5 | 2 |   |   |   |

### Riddle

**THE MORE YOU TAKE OF ME, THE MORE OF ME YOU LEAVE BEHIND. WHAT AM I?**

Footsteps

# PUZZLE #10

## (6X6)

| 1 |   |   |   |   | 1 |
|---|---|---|---|---|---|
|   |   |   |   |   |   |
|   |   |   |   |   |   |
|   | 3 |   | 4 | 3 | 2 |
|   | 4 |   | 5 |   |   |
|   |   |   |   | 2 | 5 |

**FUN FACT**

As ostrich's eye is actually bigger than its brain!

# PUZZLE #11

## (6X6)

| | | | | | 2 |
|---|---|---|---|---|---|
| 1 | | | | | |
| | | 3 | | 1 | |
| | | | | | |
| | 3 | 4 | | | 4 |
| | | | | | 2 |

# PUZZLE #12

## (7X7)

| 1 |  |  | 2 | 3 |  |  |
|---|---|---|---|---|---|---|
| 4 |  |  |  |  | 2 |  |
| 5 |  |  | 3 |  |  |  |
|  |  | 1 | 6 | 7 |  | 6 |
|  |  |  |  |  |  | 8 |
|  | 4 |  | 7 |  |  |  |
|  | 5 |  |  |  |  | 8 |

**FUN FACT**

The average human being takes in nearly eight and a half million breaths each year.

# PUZZLE #13

## (7X7)

| | 1 | | | | | 2 |
|---|---|---|---|---|---|---|
| | | | | | | 3 |
| | | 4 | | | | 5 |
| | | | 3 | 5 | | 6 |
| | | | 4 | | | 7 |
| | | | | | 8 | |
| 1 | 2 | 6 | 8 | | | 7 |

**FUN FACT**

The oldest discovered piece of chewing gum is approximately 9,000 years old and was found in Sweden!

# PUZZLE #14

## (7X7)

| 1 |   |   | 2 |   |   |   |
|---|---|---|---|---|---|---|
|   | 2 |   |   |   | 4 |   |
|   |   |   | 5 |   |   |   |
| 1 |   | 6 |   | 4 | 7 |   |
|   |   |   |   |   |   |   |
|   | 5 |   | 6 |   |   |   |
| 3 |   |   |   |   | 7 | 3 |

**FUN FACT**

A skunk can spray you from up to 12 feet away, and the stinky smell can stay on your skin up to 4 months!

# PUZZLE #15

## (7X7)

| 1 | | | | | 2 | 1 |
|---|---|---|---|---|---|---|
| 3 | | | 3 | | | |
| 4 | | | 4 | | | |
| | | | | | | |
| | 5 | 6 | | | | |
| | | | 5 | 6 | 2 | |
| | | | | | | |

# PUZZLE #16

## (7X7)

| | | | | | | 2 |
|---|---|---|---|---|---|---|
| | 3 | | | 3 | | |
| | | | | | | |
| 1 | | 4 | 5 | | | |
| | | | | | | |
| | 4 | | | | 1 | |
| | | 2 | 5 | | | |

**FUN FACT**

Humans are born with around 300 bones, but by the time they're an adult they'll only have 206.

# PATTERN RECOGNITION

Can you find the next number, letter, or shape in each of these series?

# PUZZLE #1

3  5  7  9  11  ??

# PUZZLE #2

2  4  8  16  ??  64

# PUZZLE #3

3  4  7  11  18  ??

# PUZZLE #4

2  3  10  12  13  ??

# PUZZLE #5

10  12  19  21  28  ??

# PUZZLE #6

C  D  E  F  ??  H

# PUZZLE #7

C  F  I  L  O  ??

# PUZZLE #8

ABA  BCB  CDC  ??  EFE

# PUZZLE #9

A  B  D  O  P  ??

# PUZZLE #10

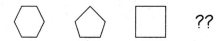 ??

# REBUS PUZZLES

A rebus puzzle hides a common English-language phrase or saying within a cryptic picture. Use clues from the picture (positioning, style, size, number, etc.) to deduce the hidden phrase in each.

# PUZZLE #1

MIL**ONE**LION

# PUZZLE #2

MAN

BOARD

# PUZZLE #3

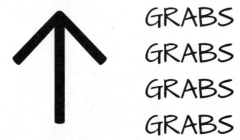

GRABS
GRABS
GRABS
GRABS

# PUZZLE #4

H      P

O      O

P      H

**FUN FACT**

Banana "trees" aren't really trees at all—they're herbs! This is because their stems contain no woody tissue.

## PUZZLE #5

```
        R
        O
R  O  A  D  S
        D
        S
```

## PUZZLE #6

TI**JUST**ME

## PUZZLE #7

‖‖READ‖‖

# PUZZLE #8

ARREST

YOU'RE

# PUZZLE #9

BAN      ANA

# PUZZLE #10

ECNALG

# PUZZLE #11

**FUN FACT**

Roughly 90% of the world's fresh water is in Antarctica ... in the form of ice!

## PUZZLE #12

**COW**

## PUZZLE #13

i i RIGHT i i

## PUZZLE #14

KNEE
LIGHTS

## PUZZLE #15

THETRUTH

# RHYMING PAIRS

We've hidden certain words in each sentence, and told you what they rhyme with. Using only that information and the context of the sentence, can you uncover each of this hidden words in these puzzles?

# PUZZLE #1

Can you find the missing words in the sentences below? Each of them rhymes with "cool".

1. Dana thought Sally was downright _ _ _ _ _ for

   pushing Pam into the swimming _ _ _ _.

2. Hal the handyman had the right _ _ _ _ to fix the

   three-legged _ _ _ _ _.

3. Ricky knew there was a _ _ _ _ against running in

   the hallways of his _ _ _ _ _ _.

# PUZZLE #2

Can you find the missing words in the sentences below? Each of them rhymes with "steal".

1. Calvin caught the snake-like _ _ _ and planned to

   cook it as tonight's _ _ _ _.

2. Tara could _ _ _ _ the pain in her _ _ _ _ when

   she knocked the back of her foot against the door.

3. Sallie let out a high-pitched _ _ _ _ _ _ of joy when

   she saw the brown _ _ _ _ wave its flippers at the

   zoo.

# PUZZLE #3

Can you find the missing words in the sentences below? Each of them rhymes with "Mabel".

1.  Without her glasses, Beatrice wasn't _ _ _ _ to read

    the washing instructions on her jacket's _ _ _ _ _.

2.  Manny hooked up the _ _ _ _ _ to his brand new

    television, but his mom insisted that he moved it off the

    kitchen _ _ _ _ _ so that everyone could eat.

3.  Gerald's favorite story was the _ _ _ _ _ of the

    horse who slept in her _ _ _ _ _ _ with a friendly

    mouse.

# PUZZLE #4

Can you find the missing words in the sentences below? Each of them rhymes with "meek".

1. The duck held a large fish in its __ __ __ __ while it was

   floating down the little __ __ __ __ __ .

2. James had a wonderful time playing hide and __ __ __ __

   with his friend from Athens, who spoke only

   __ __ __ __ __ .

3. It took Helen nearly a __ __ __ __, but after six days of

   climbing she finally made it to the top of the mountain

   __ __ __ __.

# PUZZLE #5

Can you find the missing words in the sentences below? Each of them rhymes with "tend".

1. Kristina had no money to _ _ _ _ _ on new socks, so she dug up her sewing kit and decided to _ _ _ _ her old ones instead.

2. Avery knew that Bill was a good _ _ _ _ _ _ because he was always willing to _ _ _ _ him a hand when he needed it.

3. Ally wanted to _ _ _ _ some photographs to her aunt in Alaska. To make sure they arrived intact, she wrote "Do Not _ _ _ _" on the envelope.

# SCRAMBLERS

Unscramble each of a series of words, and enter them into the squares provided—one letter per square. Then take only the numbered squares, and unscramble those letters to reveal the answer to the joke.

# PUZZLE #1

## BIRD SCRAMBLER

Try to unscramble each of the five types of birds, and write your answer in the squares provided. Then gradually fill in each numbered square at the bottom to uncover the answer to the given joke.

WKHA

ORCW

GEELA

INCALARD

GOLFMAIN

Q: What is the most expensive bird?

A: The

# PUZZLE #2

## FISH SCRAMBLER

Try to unscramble each of the six types of fish, and write your answer in the squares provided.
Then gradually fill in each numbered square at the bottom to uncover the answer to the given joke.

NATU [2][ ][ ][ ]

HKRAS [ ][3][ ][ ][ ]

OTTUR [ ][5][ ][ ][6]

MOLANS [ ][ ][ ][ ][1][ ]

DISARNE [ ][ ][ ][8][7][ ][9]

ORLUFEND [ ][ ][ ][ ][ ][4][ ]

Q: Why did the crab cross the road?

A: To get to the

[1][2][3][4][5] [6][7][8][9] !

# SHARED SEGMENTS

In each of these puzzles one segment is missing which is shared amongst each of the words listed—can you find it? The missing segment that completes each puzzle will itself be a common, one-syllable word.

# PUZZLE #1

A C _ _ _ _ _ A N T

_ _ _ _ _ _ R Y

D I S _ _ _ _ _

E N _ _ _ _ _ E R

Hint: Think of Dracula's title!

# PUZZLE #2

B _ _ _ _ _

F _ _ _ _ _ E N

C O P Y _ _ _ _ _

Hint: It's not the left . . .

# PUZZLE #3

T _ _ _ _

B _ _ _ _

D _ _ _ _

S P _ _ _ _

R E F _ _ _ _

T E R _ _ _ _

Hint: It falls from the sky ...

# PUZZLE #4

_ _ _ _ _ A L

T H O U _ _ _ _

_ _ _ _ W I C H

A M P E R _ _ _ _

Hint: You'll find this at a beach ...

# PUZZLE #5

_ _ _ _E

_ _ _ _ET

EX_ _ _ _ATION

EGG_ _ _ _T

Hint: The missing word means "to prepare for the future."

Riddle

**WHAT IS AT THE END OF EVERY RAINBOW?**
**(REMEMBER TO TURN UPSIDE DOWN TO VIEW ANSWER)**

W

# PUZZLE #6

_ _ _ _EEN

_ _ _ _ALOUPE

SIGNIFI_ _ _ _

APPLI_ _ _ _

Hint: Either you can, or you …

# PUZZLE #7

O _ _ _ _E

AR _ _ _ _E

ST_ _ _ _E

BOOME_ _ _ _

Hint: What the bell did at noon, maybe?

**FUN FACT**

Only one planet in our solar system rotates clockwise ... Venus! The rest rotate counter-clockwise.

# PUZZLE #8

AS _ _ _E

CON _ _ _E

_ _ _MARY

_ _ _MER

Hint: What you get when you add two or more numbers together ...

# PUZZLE #9

P _ _ _ R

CH _ _ _ L

ESC _ _ _ D

SH _ _ _ D

Hint: Think of King Kong …

**FUN FACT**

Koalas have fingerprints that are virtually indistinguishable from those of humans.

# PUZZLE #10

_ _ _ CH

_ _ _ TERY

_ _ _ HROOM

ACRO _ _ _

Hint: It might live in a cave …

# SUDOKU
### (4X4)

These Sudoku puzzles require the solver to complete the grid in such a way so that no number is repeated in any line (across), column (down), or 2x2 square. In these puzzles you can use only the number 1 through 4 to complete the grid.

# PUZZLE #1

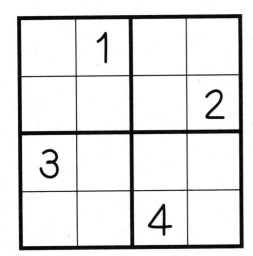

# PUZZLE #2

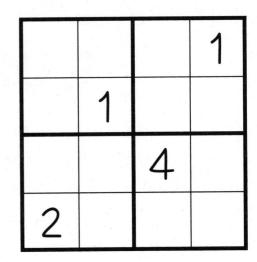

# PUZZLE #3

# PUZZLE #4

# PUZZLE #5

|   |   | 4 |   |
|---|---|---|---|
|   | 2 |   |   |
|   |   | 1 |   |
|   | 1 |   |   |

# PUZZLE #6

| 2 |   |   | 4 |
|---|---|---|---|
|   | 1 |   |   |
|   |   | 4 |   |
| 1 |   |   | 3 |

# SUDOKU
## (6X6)

These Sudoku puzzles require the solver to complete the grid in such a way so that no number is repeated in any line (across), column (down), or 2x3 rectangle. In these puzzles you can use only the number 1 through 6 to complete the grid.

# PUZZLE #1

| 4 |   | 5 |   | 6 |   |
|---|---|---|---|---|---|
| 2 |   |   |   | 5 | 3 |
|   | 4 | 1 | 5 |   |   |
|   |   | 3 | 1 | 4 |   |
| 1 | 6 |   |   |   | 5 |
| 3 |   |   |   |   | 4 |

# PUZZLE #2

| 3 | 4 |   |   |   | 6 |
|---|---|---|---|---|---|
|   |   |   | 4 | 2 |   |
|   |   |   |   | 5 | 2 |
| 2 | 5 |   | 6 |   |   |
|   | 1 | 3 |   |   | 5 |
| 5 |   |   |   | 4 |   |

# PUZZLE #3

|   |   | 2 |   | 5 | 4 |
|---|---|---|---|---|---|
|   |   |   | 6 |   |   |
| 6 |   |   | 4 |   |   |
|   |   | 4 |   |   | 2 |
|   | 4 |   |   |   |   |
| 3 | 1 |   | 2 |   |   |

# PUZZLE #4

|   |   |   |   | 3 | 2 |
|---|---|---|---|---|---|
|   |   | 3 | 6 |   |   |
|   |   | 6 |   | 2 |   |
|   | 2 |   | 1 |   |   |
|   |   | 2 | 5 |   |   |
| 6 | 3 |   |   |   |   |

## PUZZLE #5

| | 4 | | 3 | 6 | |
|---|---|---|---|---|---|
| | | | | | 4 |
| | 2 | | | 4 | |
| | 5 | | | 1 | |
| 5 | | | | | |
| | 1 | 4 | | 2 | |

## PUZZLE #6

| | 5 | | | | 4 |
|---|---|---|---|---|---|
| | 1 | | | | 5 |
| | 4 | | | | 3 |
| 3 | | | | 4 | |
| 2 | | | | 5 | |
| 5 | | | | 6 | |

## PUZZLE #7

| 2 | | 1 | 3 | | |
|---|---|---|---|---|---|
| | 3 | | | | |
| 6 | | | | 3 | |
| | 5 | | | | 1 |
| | | | | 1 | |
| | | 3 | 6 | | 4 |

## PUZZLE #8

| 6 | | | 3 | | |
|---|---|---|---|---|---|
| 4 | | | 2 | | 5 |
| | | | | | 3 |
| 1 | | | | | |
| 2 | | 4 | | | 6 |
| | | 6 | | | 2 |

# PUZZLE #9

| | 5 | | 6 | | |
|---|---|---|---|---|---|
| | | | | 1 | |
| | | 6 | | | 4 |
| 3 | | | 2 | | |
| | 2 | | | | |
| | | 3 | | 2 | |

# PUZZLE #10

| 5 | | | | 2 | 3 |
|---|---|---|---|---|---|
| | 3 | | | | 5 |
| | 2 | | | | |
| | | | 6 | | |
| 2 | | | | 5 | |
| 1 | 5 | | | | 2 |

# SUDOKU
## (9X9)

These Sudoku puzzles require the solver to complete the grid in such a way so that no number is repeated in any line (across), column (down), or 3x3 square. In these puzzles you can use only the number 1 through 9 to complete the grid.

# PUZZLE #1

| 8 | 6 | 2 |   |   |   | 5 | 1 |   |
|---|---|---|---|---|---|---|---|---|
| 3 |   | 4 | 5 | 9 |   |   |   | 2 |
|   | 9 | 5 |   | 8 |   | 7 | 3 |   |
|   | 4 |   | 7 |   | 9 | 2 |   |   |
| 9 |   |   |   | 6 |   |   |   | 3 |
|   |   | 1 |   |   | 4 |   | 7 |   |
|   | 2 | 9 |   | 1 | 8 |   | 4 |   |
| 7 | 1 |   |   | 2 | 5 | 6 |   | 8 |
|   |   |   | 9 |   |   | 1 | 2 |   |

# PUZZLE #2

| | | 2 | 3 | | 7 | 1 | 5 | |
|---|---|---|---|---|---|---|---|---|
| 8 | 1 | 5 | | 2 | | | | |
| 6 | | 7 | | | | | | 9 |
| | | 8 | 6 | | | | | 4 |
| 1 | | | 5 | 3 | 2 | | | |
| 7 | | | | | 4 | 6 | | |
| | | 9 | | | | | | 1 |
| | | | | 1 | | 5 | 8 | 6 |
| 3 | 6 | 1 | 7 | | 5 | 9 | | 2 |

# PUZZLE #3

| 5 |   |   |   |   | 6 |   |   |   |
|---|---|---|---|---|---|---|---|---|
|   |   | 6 |   |   |   |   | 2 | 1 |
|   |   | 9 | 2 | 7 | 4 |   |   | 6 |
|   |   | 2 |   | 3 |   | 9 |   |   |
|   | 3 |   |   |   |   |   | 1 |   |
|   |   | 4 |   | 8 |   | 2 |   | 3 |
| 6 | 4 |   |   | 5 | 8 | 1 |   | 2 |
| 9 | 7 |   |   |   |   | 6 |   |   |
|   |   | 1 | 7 |   |   |   |   | 8 |

# PUZZLE #4

| | | | 9 | 4 | | | 1 | 6 |
|---|---|---|---|---|---|---|---|---|
| 9 | | 7 | | 5 | | 3 | | |
| | 2 | | 3 | | | | | 8 |
| | | | | | 7 | 6 | | |
| | 8 | | | | | | 9 | |
| | | 3 | 6 | | | | | |
| 6 | | | | | 3 | | 2 | |
| | | 2 | | 6 | | 8 | | 4 |
| 7 | 1 | | | 2 | 9 | | | |

# TELEPHONE

Uncover the punch line to each of these jokes by using the telephone code in the image below. Each number in the puzzle corresponds to one of the three or four letters associated with it on a typical telephone keypad.

Remember: Each number can stand for a different letter each time it is used!

# PUZZLE #1

## WHY DID THE CHICKEN CROSS THE PLAYGROUND?

$\overline{8}\,\overline{6}$  $\overline{4}\,\overline{3}\,\overline{8}$  $\overline{8}\,\overline{6}$  $\overline{8}\,\overline{4}\,\overline{3}$

$\overline{6}\,\overline{8}\,\overline{4}\,\overline{3}\,\overline{7}$  $\overline{7}\,\overline{5}\,\overline{4}\,\overline{3}\,\overline{3}$ .

# PUZZLE #2

## WHY WAS 6 AFRAID OF 7?

$\overline{2}\,\overline{3}\,\overline{2}\,\overline{2}\,\overline{8}\,\overline{7}\,\overline{3}$  $\overline{7}\,\overline{3}\,\overline{8}\,\overline{3}\,\overline{6}$

$\overline{2}\,\overline{8}\,\overline{3}$  $\overline{6}\,\overline{4}\,\overline{6}\,\overline{3}$ .

# PUZZLE #3

## DID YOU HEAR ABOUT THE DOG THAT WENT TO THE FLEA CIRCUS?

$\overline{4}\,\overline{3}$  $\overline{7}\,\overline{8}\,\overline{6}\,\overline{5}\,\overline{3}$  $\overline{8}\,\overline{4}\,\overline{3}$

$\overline{7}\,\overline{4}\,\overline{6}\,\overline{9}$ .

# PUZZLE #4

## WHY ARE SPIDERS SUCH GOOD SWIMMERS?

$\overline{8}\,\overline{4}\,\overline{3}\,\overline{9}$  $\overline{4}\,\overline{2}\,\overline{8}\,\overline{3}$

$\overline{9}\,\overline{3}\,\overline{2}\,\overline{2}\,\overline{3}\,\overline{3}$  $\overline{3}\,\overline{3}\,\overline{3}\,\overline{8}$ .

# PUZZLE #5

## WHAT HAS A TRUNK AND IS SEEN AT THE NORTH POLE?

$\overline{2}$  $\overline{5}$ $\overline{6}$ $\overline{7}$ $\overline{8}$

$\overline{3}$ $\overline{5}$ $\overline{3}$ $\overline{7}$ $\overline{4}$ $\overline{2}$ $\overline{6}$ $\overline{8}$ .

# PUZZLE #6

## WHAT DID ONE PENCIL SAY TO THE OTHER?

$\overline{9}$ $\overline{6}$ $\overline{8}$  $\overline{2}$ $\overline{7}$ $\overline{3}$

$\overline{5}$ $\overline{6}$ $\overline{6}$ $\overline{5}$ $\overline{4}$ $\overline{6}$ $\overline{4}$  $\overline{7}$ $\overline{4}$ $\overline{2}$ $\overline{7}$ $\overline{7}$ .

# PUZZLE #7

## WHY DO GOLFERS ALWAYS WEAR TWO SHIRTS?

$\overline{4}$ $\overline{6}$  $\overline{2}$ $\overline{2}$ $\overline{7}$ $\overline{3}$  $\overline{8}$ $\overline{4}$ $\overline{3}$ $\overline{9}$

$\overline{4}$ $\overline{3}$ $\overline{8}$  $\overline{2}$  $\overline{4}$ $\overline{6}$ $\overline{5}$ $\overline{3}$

$\overline{4}$ $\overline{6}$  $\overline{6}$ $\overline{6}$ $\overline{3}$ .

# PUZZLE #8

## WHAT CAN TRAVEL ALL OVER THE WORLD WITHOUT EVER LEAVING ITS CORNER?

$\overline{2}$ $\overline{7}$ $\overline{6}$ $\overline{7}$ $\overline{8}$ $\overline{2}$ $\overline{4}$ $\overline{3}$

$\overline{7}$ $\overline{8}$ $\overline{2}$ $\overline{6}$ $\overline{7}$ .

# PUZZLE #9

## WHERE DOES FROSTY THE SNOW MAN STORE HIS MONEY?

$\overline{4}$ $\overline{6}$ $\overline{2}$

$\overline{7}$ $\overline{6}$ $\overline{6}$ $\overline{9}$ $\overline{2}$ $\overline{2}$ $\overline{6}$ $\overline{5}$ .

# PUZZLE #10

## WHY DID THE TRIANGLE GIVE UP TRYING TO BECOME A CIRCLE?

$\overline{4}$ $\overline{3}$ $\overline{5}$ $\overline{6}$ $\overline{3}$ $\overline{9}$ $\overline{4}$ $\overline{8}$

$\overline{9}$ $\overline{2}$ $\overline{7}$ $\overline{7}$ $\overline{6}$ $\overline{4}$ $\overline{6}$ $\overline{8}$ $\overline{5}$ $\overline{3}$ $\overline{7}$ $\overline{7}$ .

# VOWELLESS

Vowelless puzzles contain five words, each of which is related to a given theme. All the vowels (A, E, I, O, and U) have been removed from each word. Can you figure out what all five words are?

# PUZZLE #1

## REPTILES

SNK _ _ _ _ _ _

CRCDL _ _ _ _ _ _ _ _ _ _

LZRD _ _ _ _ _ _

LLGTR _ _ _ _ _ _ _ _ _

GN _ _ _ _ _ _

# PUZZLE #2

## COUNTRIES

FRNC _ _ _ _ _ _ _

CND _ _ _ _ _ _

MXC _ _ _ _ _ _

TLY _ _ _ _ _

ND _ _ _ _ _

# PUZZLE #3
## PRESIDENTS

WSHNGTN __ __ __ __ __ __ __ __ __ __

LNCLN __ __ __ __ __ __ __

KNNDY __ __ __ __ __ __ __

SNHWR __ __ __ __ __ __ __ __ __ __

DMS __ __ __ __ __ __

# PUZZLE #4
## COLORS

GRN __ __ __ __ __ __

YLLW __ __ __ __ __ __ __

VLT __ __ __ __ __ __ __

RNG __ __ __ __ __ __ __

NDG __ __ __ __ __ __ __

# PUZZLE #5

## VEGETABLES

BRCCL _ _ _ _ _ _ _ _ _

CRRT _ _ _ _ _ _

GGPLNT _ _ _ _ _ _ _ _

PTT _ _ _ _ _ _

NN _ _ _ _ _

# PUZZLE #6

## METALS

SLVR _ _ _ _ _ _

CPPR _ _ _ _ _ _

BRNZ _ _ _ _ _ _

TTNM _ _ _ _ _ _ _ _

RN _ _ _ _

# PUZZLE #7
## MAMMALS

SQRRL  _ _ _ _ _ _ _ _ _

BVR  _ _ _ _ _ _ _

WLRS  _ _ _ _ _ _ _

LPHNT  _ _ _ _ _ _ _ _

TTR  _ _ _ _ _ _

# PUZZLE #8
## MONTHS

JNRY  _ _ _ _ _ _ _ _

JN  _ _ _ _

CTBR  _ _ _ _ _ _ _ _

PRL  _ _ _ _ _

GST  _ _ _ _ _ _

# PUZZLE #9

## WORDS MEANING "BIG"

LRG _ _ _ _ _ _

GGNTC _ _ _ _ _ _ _ _ _

HG _ _ _ _ _

NRMS _ _ _ _ _ _ _ _ _

MMNS _ _ _ _ _ _ _ _

# PUZZLE #10

## PLANETS

JPTR _ _ _ _ _ _ _ _

MRCRY _ _ _ _ _ _ _ _

NPTN _ _ _ _ _ _ _ _

RTH _ _ _ _ _ _

RNS _ _ _ _ _ _ _

# WORD BLOCKS

Each Word Block puzzle contains six nine-letter words (each with four letters missing) on the left, and six four-letter words on the right. Each of the words on the right fits into one, and only one, spot in the list on the left. See if you can complete every nine-letter word by matching them correctly!

# PUZZLE #1

| A | N | E | C |  |  |  |  | S |
|---|---|---|---|---|---|---|---|---|
| D | E | V | E |  |  |  |  | D |
| R | E |  |  |  |  | D | E | R |
| C | O | M |  |  |  |  | E | E |
| C | O | N |  |  |  |  | R | S |
| A | D |  |  |  |  | B | L | E |

| M | I | T | T |
|---|---|---|---|
| S | I | D | E |
| D | O | T | E |
| L | O | P | E |
| V | I | S | A |
| M | A | I | N |

# PUZZLE #2

| C | H | O |  |  |  |  | T | E |
|---|---|---|---|---|---|---|---|---|
| C | O | N |  |  |  |  | O | R |
| S | W |  |  |  |  |  | I | N | G |
| I | N | S |  |  |  |  | E | D |
| A | F |  |  |  |  | O | O | N |
| N | E | T |  |  |  |  | E | D |

| T | A | L | L |
|---|---|---|---|
| W | O | R | K |
| T | E | R | N |
| I | T | C | H |
| C | O | L | A |
| D | U | C | T |

## PUZZLE #3

```
S E _ _ _ _ I N G          C E N T
E C _ _ _ _ R I C          A R C H
C O L _ _ _ _ E D          M A N E
P E R _ _ _ N T            L A P S
C _ _ _ _ A L E D          P O L O
A _ _ _ _ G I E S          O N C E
```

## PUZZLE #4

```
F U L _ _ _ _ E D          H O N E
D I S _ _ _ _ S T          M E N S
D I _ _ _ _ I O N          T E R M
A P _ _ _ _ I N G          T I M E
D E _ _ _ _ I N E          P E A L
S E N _ _ _ N T            F I L L
```

## PUZZLE #5

```
V A R I _ _ _ S        L O N G
A _ _ _ S I D E        S P I T
A D _ _ _ I O N        A B L E
C U R _ _ _ L Y        M I S S
P R E _ _ _ N T        R E N T
H O _ _ _ A L S        S I D E
```

## PUZZLE #6

```
L _ _ _ _ C A P E      P I N E
H I E R _ _ _ Y        C H I N
A T T A _ _ _ G        L I V E
D E _ _ _ R E D        M U S E
A _ _ _ M E N T        A R C H
H A P _ _ _ S S        A N D S
```

## PUZZLE #7

| E | X |  |  |  |  | E | N | T |
|---|---|---|---|---|---|---|---|---|
| A | C |  |  |  |  | I | N | G |
| H | O | P | E |  |  |  | Y |  |
| C | H | E |  |  |  | R | Y |  |
| A | N |  |  |  | C | E | D |  |
| I | M |  |  |  | A | N | T |  |

| N | O | U | N |
|---|---|---|---|
| F | U | L | L |
| P | O | R | T |
| C | E | L | L |
| C | O | R | D |
| M | I | S | T |

## PUZZLE #8

| A |  |  |  | O | N | E | D |
|---|---|---|---|---|---|---|---|
| B |  |  |  | M | A | I | L |
| E | M |  |  |  | E | E | S |
| A | T |  |  |  | I | O | N |
| C | U | S |  |  |  | R | S |
| P | O | R |  |  |  | E | D |

| L | A | C | K |
|---|---|---|---|
| T | R | A | Y |
| T | O | M | E |
| P | L | O | Y |
| T | E | N | T |
| B | A | N | D |

## PUZZLE #9

```
D I S [ ] [ ] [ ] R S      D U A L
G R A [ ] [ ] [ ] L Y      V E N T
S T R [ ] [ ] [ ] E D      T R O D
S U S [ ] [ ] [ ] E D      C O V E
I N [ ] [ ] [ ] U C E      E T C H
A D [ ] [ ] [ ] U R E      P E N D
```

## PUZZLE #10

```
C O N [ ] [ ] [ ] E D      P O K E
C [ ] [ ] [ ] E N G E      L I C E
P O [ ] [ ] [ ] M A N      T U N A
S [ ] [ ] [ ] S M A N      V E R Y
F O R [ ] [ ] [ ] T E      F I R M
E [ ] [ ] [ ] B O D Y      H A L L
```

# WORD LADDERS

Can you complete each "word ladder" by changing just one letter to make a new word that fits the given definitions? Remember, only one letter will change from each word to the next!

# PUZZLE #1

## S E L F

_ _ _ _
Opposite of buy

_ _ _ _
Took a tumble

_ _ _ _
Leaf-turning season

## F A I L

# PUZZLE #2

## L O V E

_ _ _ _
Bird symbolizing peace

_ _ _ _
Jump into a pool

_ _ _ _
Coin worth 10 cents

## T I M E

## PUZZLE #3

### T U B A

___ ___ ___ ___

Large ocean fish

___ ___ ___ ___

Adjust a piano

___ ___ ___ ___

Dial ___ (phone sound)

### B O N E

## PUZZLE #4

### W A N T

___ ___ ___ ___

Breathe like a dog

___ ___ ___ ___

Half a quart

___ ___ ___ ___

Fragrant tree

### P I L E

# PUZZLE #5

## Y E A R

\_\_ \_\_ \_\_ \_\_

Winnie the Pooh is one

\_\_ \_\_ \_\_ \_\_

Prepare raw eggs

\_\_ \_\_ \_\_ \_\_

Red root vegetable

## M E E T

# PUZZLE #6

## G O A L S

\_\_ \_\_ \_\_ \_\_ \_\_

Bearded farm animals

\_\_ \_\_ \_\_ \_\_ \_\_

Vessels on the water

\_\_ \_\_ \_\_ \_\_ \_\_

Cowboy's footwear

## B O O T H

# PUZZLE #7

## D A I R Y

___ ___ ___ ___ ___
Tinker Bell is one

___ ___ ___ ___ ___
Annual county festivals

___ ___ ___ ___ ___
Doesn't succeed

## F A L L S

# PUZZLE #8

## B U T L E R

___ ___ ___ ___ ___ ___
Popcorn topping

___ ___ ___ ___ ___ ___
Pancake mixture

___ ___ ___ ___ ___ ___
Be important

## M A S T E R

## PUZZLE #9

B O X E R

— — — — —
What gifts come in

— — — — —
Parts of a skeleton

— — — — —
Ice cream holders

C A N E S

## PUZZLE #10

W H O L E

— — — — —
During

— — — — —
Groan and complain

— — — — —
"Rise and ____!"

S H I N Y

# WORD SEARCH

We've given you a grid of *seemingly-random* letters, but hidden within each is one or more words written either horizontally, vertically, or diagonally ... and sometimes in reverse! See if you can find them all!

# PUZZLE #1

## YOU'LL GO BANANAS!

This word search puzzle is a bit different from the rest ... there's only a single word hidden within it. See if you find the word "Banana" once (and only once!) in the grid below.

```
N A N A N N B A A N B
A B N N A A A A B N N
A A A B A B N N A A B
N A B N B A B A A N A
A N N B A N A B B A N
A B A A A B A N B N
N A A N B N B A A N A
B B A B A B A B N A A
N A N A B N A N A N B
B N A N A A N A A B A
N B N N A B A A B A N
```

# PUZZLE #2

## NUMBER FIND

We've drawn a series of numbers on this page. See if you can find each of them (spelled out, of course!) in the word search grid below.

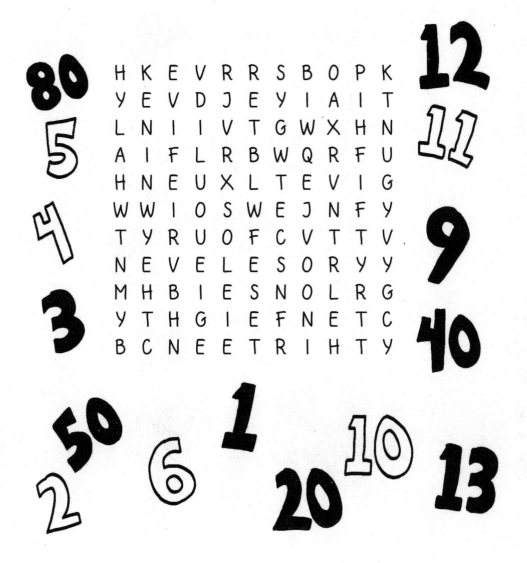

80
12
5
11
4
9
3
40

H K E V R R S B O P K
Y E V D J E Y I A I T
L N I I V T G W X H N
A I F L R B W Q R F U
H N E U X L T E V I G
W W I O S W E J N F Y
T Y R U O F C V T T V
N E V E L E S O R Y Y
M H B I E S N O L R G
Y T H G I E F N E T C
B C N E E T R I H T Y

50
1
10
2
6
20
13

# PUZZLE #3

## COUNTRIES OF THE WORLD

Can you find all 10 of the countries shown on this page in the word search grid below?

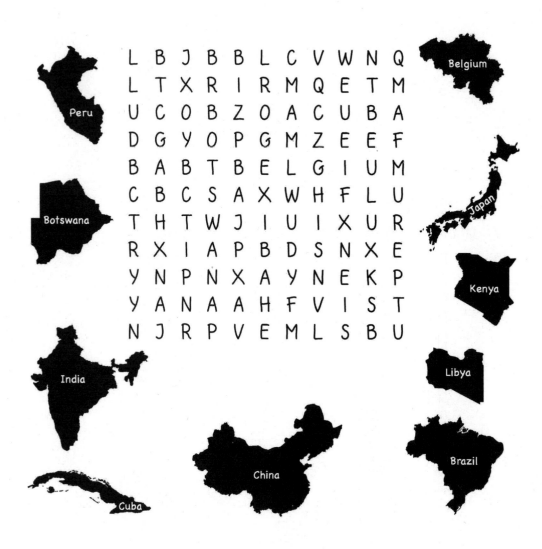

```
L B J B B L C V W N Q
L T X R I R M Q E T M
U C O B Z O A C U B A
D G Y O P G M Z E E F
B A B T B E L G I U M
C B C S A X W H F L U
T H T W J I U I X U R
R X I A P B D S N X E
Y N P N X A Y N E K P
Y A N A A H F V I S T
N J R P V E M L S B U
```

Peru

Belgium

Botswana

Japan

Kenya

India

Libya

Cuba

China

Brazil

# PUZZLE #4

## HUNTING FOR ANIMALS

Can you find all eight of the animals shown on this page in the word search grid below? The number shown next to each animal tells you how many letters is in each answer.

# PUZZLE #5

## CREEPY CRAWLIES

See if you can find all of these "creepy crawlies" in the word search grid below!

```
T O D R A G O N F L Y
E T T M Q F D Z W A A
K I A T N A B Q G L R
C U L E R H D C L E N
I Q P D L B J L D T O
R S S Q E F T I K V I
C O A E M U P M H C P
Y M W H O S H W N R R
I B U T T E R F L Y O
J G M B H M U F T H C
C E N T I P E D E R S
```

| Ant | Flea |
| Bee | Mosquito |
| Butterfly | Moth |
| Centipede | Scorpion |
| Cricket | Spider |
| Dragonfly | Wasp |

# PUZZLE #6

## FIND THE STATES

```
A N E W Y O R K E I N D I A N A
N A R V D U F L E Y I B N K W R
A D T G U A Z Y S Q S A A L Q E
T G L O H I O W S V N W U O I G
N O E A K A O R E G O N E O G A
O F T O H A D I N I C N G W M D
M U V Y R K D I N S S E P A U X
E N I A M G M H E X I V B P S X
S A X E T O I W T F W A M R E H
X Y I E Y B D A A R L D J Z G N
I I A W A H F B J A O A I Q J L
H S I O N I L L I K A N S A S Z
```

| | | |
|---|---|---|
| Alabama | Kansas | Oregon |
| Georgia | Maine | Tennessee |
| Hawaii | Montana | Texas |
| Idaho | Nevada | Utah |
| Illinois | New York | Wisconsin |
| Indiana | North Dakota | Wyoming |
| Iowa | Ohio | |

# PUZZLE #7

## IN THE CLASSROOM

Can you find all 17 items (each commonly found in a classroom) in the word search grid below?

```
N O T E B O O K E K B Q W B M L
S R O S S I C S C O O X S L R R
G I R Q V Y O O D E S K I Q E T
B V H E R G L S F N W C X T B A
A P S R L C T L J Q N P U L O F
C G A A L U A B J E O P G H F T
K E B S D G R T P F M A P P L E
P N G E D I C T I O N A R Y T M
A X N R U M D H C T E A C H E R
C T T S N H C H A L K B O A R D
K P M J J I P J D I T C E E A S
R O T A L U C L A C R Z F E P B
```

| | | | |
|---|---|---|---|
| Apple | Clock | Flag | Student |
| Backpack | Computer | Notebook | Teacher |
| Calculator | Desk | Pencil | |
| Chair | Dictionary | Ruler | |
| Chalkboard | Eraser | Scissors | |

# PUZZLE #8

## CAMPING TRIP

All of the terms listed here are things you might see on a typical camping trip. Can you find them all in the grid below?

```
I D T L J W T H A M M O C K X D
Z T L S B N F L A S H L I G H T
C D T I E W L H H Y F E P Z D N
T A H T A T F Y X D K F H K Q L
P N M M A R S H M A L L O W T O
E A M R M K T R L C O M P A S S
O E M Z O W I L D L I F E Q T E
N E C A M P S I T E E Y Y U V Y
A E J L U T E L I R U B P O R T
C R R H O W I X I L A N T E R N
U T H O A M O F O R E S T B L F
Q Q B I K C M H B A C K P A C K
```

| Backpack | Fire | Lake | Stove |
| --- | --- | --- | --- |
| Boots | Flashlight | Lantern | Tent |
| Campsite | Forest | Map | Trail |
| Canoe | Hammock | Marshmallow | Tree |
| Compass | Hat | Rope | Wildlife |

# PUZZLE #9

## TRICK OR TREAT!

You'll have a spooky fun time searching for all of these Halloween-themed words in the grid below!

```
N S E M U T S O C C U Q H W W Z
I K F G W V G M B J P A M H E I
K V C B P G A A Q O W I T C H C
P Y V I E E T F X E E G D V P H
M T L D R A Y E V A R G H G N Y
U R D C O T I C R Q E R G O M S
P A S Z S P I D E R W E B M S Z
A P O V A M P I R E O T U I Y T
S K E L E T O N E G L M R D D V
R E T S N O M O D X F J N E S H
Z C G H X T J D N I U A E Q A G
M O P D L B L A C K C A T V I T
```

| Bat | Graveyard | Pumpkin | Trick |
|-----|-----------|---------|-------|
| Black cat | Monster | Scream | Vampire |
| Candy | Moon | Skeleton | Werewolf |
| Costume | Mummy | Spider web | Witch |
| Ghost | Party | Treat | |

# PUZZLE #10

## WE ALL SCREAM FOR ICE CREAM

Find all these ice cream flavors in the grid below. But take your time—you don't want to get an ice cream headache!

```
N P R N V I T R O C K Y R O A D
R A E G B N E J R L T G S W J Z
J U J A I D B J E A U C G Y U L
C G M M N A W E V A N I L L A X
I Y W R N U F B E P O X C L T T
N S J A A F T C H O C O L A T E
N P N H O I A B V M O H O R M J
A A E T B L S D U A C E E M F N
M Y B A B V H I X T F M Q R R B
O Y E N C C K H N Q T P M J R R
N V A M S H B U B B L E G U M Y
Y E O I H C A T S I P X R S T D
```

Banana
Bubble gum
Cherry
Chocolate
Cinnamon
Coconut
Mint

Peach
Peanut butter
Pistachio
Rocky road
Rum raisin
Toffee
Vanilla

# WORDS OUT OF WORDS

One long "master word" is given at the top of each of these puzzles. Your task is to use only the letters in that word to spell out the answers to each of the clues provided. You can use each letter only once, unless it appears more than once in the master word (i.e., the "R" in RHINOCEROS can be used up to two times in each answer). Good luck!

# PUZZLE #1

# R H I N O C E R O S

_ _ _ _ _
Cowboy's ride, often

_ _ _ _ _
Nickels, quarters, and dimes

_ _ _ _ _
Black and white cream-filled cookies

_ _ _ _ _ _
Twelve of these make a foot

_ _ _ _ _ _
Little Jack Horner sat in a _____

Riddle

**WHAT BUILDING HAS MORE THAN 500 STORIES?**

A library

# PUZZLE #2

# OUTER SPACE

$\underline{\quad}\ \underline{\quad}\ \underline{\quad}\ \underline{\quad}\ \underline{\quad}$
What a volcano does

$\underline{\quad}\ \underline{\quad}\ \underline{\quad}\ \underline{\quad}\ \underline{\quad}$
Cast member in a movie

$\underline{\quad}\ \underline{\quad}\ \underline{\quad}\ \underline{\quad}\ \underline{\quad}$
Use the pink part of a pencil

$\underline{\quad}\ \underline{\quad}\ \underline{\quad}\ \underline{\quad}\ \underline{\quad}\ \underline{\quad}$
Flying _____ (U.F.O.)

$\underline{\quad}\ \underline{\quad}\ \underline{\quad}\ \underline{\quad}\ \underline{\quad}\ \underline{\quad}$
Roller _____ (theme park ride)

**FUN FACT**

There are more plastic flamingos in the United States than there are real flamingos!

# MINNESOTA

_ _ _ _ _

You can skip one over water

_ _ _ _ _

Very hot water vapor

_ _ _ _ _

Horses have these on their necks

_ _ _ _ _ _

Game with rackets and a net

_ _ _ _ _ _ _

Rich person's house, maybe

# PUZZLE #4

# ARITHMETIC

_ _ _ _ _ _

Trick or _____!

_ _ _ _ _ _

Valentine's Day symbol

_ _ _ _ _ _

A certain month

_ _ _ _ _

Planet where we all live

_ _ _ _ _ _ _

Crab that often changes shells

# PUZZLE #5

# SUBMARINE

_ _ _ _ _

Goldilocks and the Three _____

_ _ _ _ _

Hospital worker

_ _ _ _ _

What the Scarecrow lacked

_ _ _ _ _ _

Three, five, or twelve

_ _ _ _ _ _

Black-and-blue injury

### Riddle

**WHAT WORD STARTS WITH AN "E" AND ENDS WITH AN "E", BUT HAS ONLY ONE LETTER IN IT?**

An envelope

# PUZZLE #6

# TRAMPOLINE

\_ \_ \_ \_ \_

Instrument with black and white keys

\_ \_ \_ \_ \_

Boss of an airline cockpit

\_ \_ \_ \_ \_ \_

Mother or father

\_ \_ \_ \_ \_

Multiply by three

\_ \_ \_ \_ \_ \_

Venus, Mars, or Jupiter

Riddle

WHAT HAS TWO HANDS AND A FACE, BUT NO LEGS OR FEET?

A clock

# PUZZLE #7

# T A N G E R I N E

_ _ _ _ _ _

Blue mixed with yellow

_ _ _ _ _ _

Big striped cat

_ _ _ _ _

Bottle dweller that grants wishes

_ _ _ _ _ _

Front part of a train

_ _ _ _ _ _ _ _

Any whole number

# PUZZLE #8

# PAINTBRUSH

_ _ _ _ _
Mom's sisters

_ _ _ _ _
Like a knife's edge

_ _ _ _ _
What a nun wears

_ _ _ _ _ _
Run really, really fast

_ _ _ _ _ _
Discipline for bad behavior

# PUZZLE #9

# LONGITUDE

\_ \_ \_ \_ \_ \_

Opposite of innocence

\_ \_ \_ \_ \_ \_

Fabled type of goose egg

\_ \_ \_ \_ \_ \_

Where your taste buds are

\_ \_ \_ \_ \_ \_

First part of "U.S.A."

\_ \_ \_ \_ \_ \_

Worked very hard

**FUN FACT**

A group of lions is called a pride. A group of kangaroos is called a troop. And a group of jellyfish is called a smack!

# PUZZLE #10

# SALAMANDER

— — — — —
It wakes you up in the morning

— — — — —
Sleep phenomenon

— — — — —
Olympic gold, silver, or bronze

— — — — —
Leafy green meal starter

— — — — — —
Type of open-toed footwear

**FUN FACT**

Zebra stripes are like human fingerprints ... no two zebras share the exact same pattern!

# SOLUTIONS

## ACROSTICS

### PUZZLE #1

"Life itself is the most wonderful fairy tale."— Hans Christen Andersen

| | |
|---|---|
| STIFF | RULER |
| LION | HIDE |
| TOWEL | METAL |
| FIFTY | SEAS |

### PUZZLE #2

"Why fit in when you were born to stand out?"—Dr. Seuss

| | |
|---|---|
| FORTY | RUINED |
| TWENTY | ONION |
| WOW | HEAT |
| BUSH | |

### PUZZLE #3

"It doesn't matter how slowly you go - as long as you don't stop!"—Confucius

| | |
|---|---|
| MONOPOLY | OWLS |
| GRADUATE | HOOT |
| SNOW | NASTY |
| GOOSE | TILT |
| STUDY | |

### PUZZLE #4

"Weeds are flowers too, once you get to know them."—A.A. Milne

| | |
|---|---|
| GOOFY | TOWN |
| KNEW | HEEL |
| TREES | TOAD |
| COW | TORE |
| MOUSE | |

# ACROSTICS

## PUZZLE #5

"No act of kindness, no matter how small, is ever wasted."—Aesop

MONTHS      ODD
WORM      CATS
WRIST      LEAF
NAIL      SOAK
SEVENTEEN

## PUZZLE #6

"A journey of a thousand miles begins with a single step."—Proverb

BEAUTY      FALL
JIGSAW      SEED
SPOON      RISE
NEST      HIGH
MOUNTAIN

## PUZZLE #7

"The most beautiful adventures are not those we go to seek."—Robert Louis Stevenson

SWEET      GUARD
EARTH      TEST
SLEEVE      TOOTH
BIKE      UNSAFE
OUT      MOON

## PUZZLE #8

"The only way to have a friend is to be one."—Ralph Waldo Emerson

HONEY      BOAT
LEFT      NINETY
SHOW      AREA
VIDEO

## PUZZLE #9

"A person who has good thoughts cannot ever be ugly."—Roald Dahl

EGGS      VOWELS
BANANA      THEY
POOH      CUTE
THORN      DOGS
HOUR

## PUZZLE #10

"The secret of getting ahead is getting started."—Mark Twain

EIGHTEEN      EAST
TIGHT      FEET
GRADE      CARD
STING      TOTS

# BUTTERFLY MATH

### PUZZLE #1

= 5

= 2

= 3

### PUZZLE #2

= 3

= 4

= 9

### PUZZLE #3

= 7

= 3

= 4

= 14

### PUZZLE #4

= 3

= 1

= 2

= 6

### PUZZLE #5

= 4

= 6

= 7

= 12

# CLUELESS CROSSWORDS

**PUZZLE #1**

| | | | | |
|---|---|---|---|---|
| 1 = T | 7 = R | 13 = P | 19 = Y | 25 = H |
| 2 = Z | 8 = L | 14 = N | 20 = J | 26 = U |
| 3 = W | 9 = Q | 15 = F | 21 = M | |
| 4 = D | 10 = I | 16 = G | 22 = C | |
| 5 = V | 11 = K | 17 = X | 23 = B | |
| 6 = O | 12 = A | 18 = S | 24 = E | |

**PUZZLE #2**

| | | | | |
|---|---|---|---|---|
| 1 = J | 7 = N | 13 = H | 19 = W | 25 = G |
| 2 = T | 8 = X | 14 = B | 20 = O | 26 = Q |
| 3 = A | 9 = E | 15 = U | 21 = M | |
| 4 = R | 10 = K | 16 = C | 22 = S | |
| 5 = P | 11 = I | 17 = V | 23 = Z | |
| 6 = L | 12 = Y | 18 = F | 24 = D | |

**PUZZLE #3**

| | | | | |
|---|---|---|---|---|
| 1 = P | 7 = K | 13 = W | 19 = Z | 25 = S |
| 2 = O | 8 = B | 14 = Q | 20 = I | 26 = V |
| 3 = C | 9 = E | 15 = Y | 21 = X | |
| 4 = F | 10 = N | 16 = U | 22 = J | |
| 5 = R | 11 = M | 17 = T | 23 = G | |
| 6 = L | 12 = D | 18 = H | 24 = A | |

**PUZZLE #4**

| | | | | |
|---|---|---|---|---|
| 1 = M | 7 = Q | 13 = S | 19 = V | 25 = O |
| 2 = D | 8 = I | 14 = L | 20 = H | 26 = W |
| 3 = N | 9 = A | 15 = B | 21 = P | |
| 4 = E | 10 = Z | 16 = C | 22 = G | |
| 5 = Y | 11 = F | 17 = X | 23 = K | |
| 6 = T | 12 = J | 18 = U | 24 = R | |

**PUZZLE #5**

| | | | | |
|---|---|---|---|---|
| 1 = Y | 7 = G | 13 = U | 19 = E | 25 = F |
| 2 = A | 8 = M | 14 = C | 20 = V | 26 = D |
| 3 = B | 9 = L | 15 = K | 21 = W | |
| 4 = I | 10 = Z | 16 = Q | 22 = O | |
| 5 = N | 11 = H | 17 = X | 23 = T | |
| 6 = P | 12 = J | 18 = S | 24 = R | |

# CRAZY CODES

**PUZZLE #1**

**PUZZLE #2**

Triangle. There are 11 triangles, 10 hexagons, 9 circles, 8 pentagons, and 4 squares.

**PUZZLE #3**

There are 6 different shapes:

**PUZZLE #4**

There are 12 different aliens. This one appears only once.

**PUZZLE #5**

There are six different types of cat. This cat appears only three times:

**PUZZLE #6**

This flower and pot combination appears the most (9 times):

**PUZZLE #7**

This robot appears only once:

# CROSSWORDS

### PUZZLE #1

### PUZZLE #2

### PUZZLE #3

### PUZZLE #4

### PUZZLE #5

### PUZZLE #6

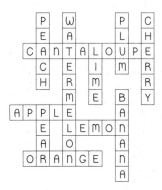

# CROSSWORDS

### PUZZLE #7

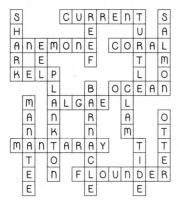

### PUZZLE #8

### PUZZLE #9

### PUZZLE #10

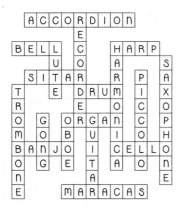

# CRYPTOGRAMS

### PUZZLE #1

"We make a living by what we get, but we make a life by what we give."

### PUZZLE #2

"Anyone who has never made a mistake has never tried anything new."

### PUZZLE #3

"The only sure thing about luck is that it will change."

### PUZZLE #4

"The future belongs to those who believe in the beauty of their dreams."
—Eleanor Roosevelt

### PUZZLE #5

"Never fear shadows. They simply mean that there's a light somewhere nearby."
—Ruth E. Renkei

### PUZZLE #6

"The first step toward greatness is to be honest."
—Proverb

### PUZZLE #7

"You will never do anything in this world without courage."
—Aristotle

### PUZZLE #8

"Learn as much as you can while you are young, since life becomes too busy later."
—Dana Stewart Scott

### PUZZLE #9

"A child can ask questions that a wise man cannot answer."
—Proverb

### PUZZLE #10

"Education's purpose is to replace an empty mind with an open one."
—Malcolm S. Forbes

# CRYPTOGRAMS

## PUZZLE #11

"You don't have to be great to start but you have to start to be great."
—Zig Ziglar

## PUZZLE #12

"You are braver than you believe, stronger than you seem and smarter than you think."
—A.A. Milne

## PUZZLE #13

"All your dreams can come true if you have the courage to pursue them."
—Walt Disney

## PUZZLE #14

"Don't cry because it's over, smile because it happened."
—Dr. Seuss

## PUZZLE #15

"It is better to be a failure at something you love than to be a success at something you hate."
—George Burns

## PUZZLE #16

"I knew who I was this morning but I've changed a few times since then."
—Lewis Carroll

## PUZZLE #17

"If you want your dreams to come true, don't oversleep."
—Proverb

## PUZZLE #18

"A little nonsense now and then, is cherished by the wisest men."
—Roald Dahl

## PUZZLE #19

"It is our choices that show what we truly are, far more than our abilities."
—J.K. Rowling

## PUZZLE #20

"An ounce of practice is worth a pound of preaching."
—Proverb

# DOT TO DOT

**PUZZLE #1**

**PUZZLE #2**

**PUZZLE #3**

**PUZZLE #4**

# DOT TO DOT

### PUZZLE #5

### PUZZLE #6

### PUZZLE #7

### PUZZLE #8

### PUZZLE #9

### PUZZLE #10

# DROP QUOTES

### PUZZLE #1  PUBLILIUS SYRUS
No one knows what he can do until he tries.

### PUZZLE #2  PROVERB
The grass is always greener on the other side.

### PUZZLE #3  J.K. ROWLING
We all must make the choice between what is right, and what is easy.

### PUZZLE #4  HENRY FORD
Whether you think you can, or think you can't, you're right.

### PUZZLE #5  LEWIS CARROLL
Sometimes, I've believed as many as six impossible things before breakfast.

### PUZZLE #6  JOHN HAYS HAMMOND
Character is the real foundation of all worthwhile success.

### PUZZLE #7  PROVERB
When the going gets tough, the tough get going.

### PUZZLE #8  AESOP
No act of kindness, no matter how small, is ever wasted.

### PUZZLE #9  WALT DISNEY
Our greatest natural resource is the minds of our children.

### PUZZLE #10  DR. SEUSS
Be who you are and say what you feel, because those who mind don't matter and those who matter don't mind.

# ELIMINATION QUOTES

### PUZZLE #1

If you can dream it, you can do it!
—Walt Disney

### PUZZLE #2

I am not young enough to know everything.
—Oscar wilde

### PUZZLE #3

The truth is always the strongest argument.
—Sophocles

### PUZZLE #4

Adults are just children who earn money.
—Kenneth Branaugh

### PUZZLE #5

Fantasy is a necessary ingredient in living.
—Dr. Seuss

# LOGIC PUZZLES

### PUZZLE #1 - THROWING DARTS

| | | |
|---|---|---|
| 41 | Hubert | black |
| 48 | Felix | violet |
| 55 | Shaun | red |
| 62 | Matthew | green |

### PUZZLE #2 - ATHLETE OF THE YEAR

| | | |
|---|---|---|
| 4 | Pablo | basketball |
| 11 | Ken | soccer |
| 18 | Colin | football |
| 25 | Tommy | hockey |

### PUZZLE #3 - THE FUN RUN

| | | |
|---|---|---|
| 21 minutes | Anthony | pink |
| 22 minutes | Orlando | orange |
| 23 minutes | Ralph | blackv |
| 24 minutes | Daryl | red |
| 25 minutes | Patrick | silver |

### PUZZLE #4 - PETE'S PET STORE

| | | |
|---|---|---|
| January | Olivia | macaw |
| February | Sara | canary |
| March | Pam | lovebird |
| April | Velma | parrot |
| May | Ida | lorikeet |

### PUZZLE #5 - THE WORLD'S RICHEST PEOPLE

| | | |
|---|---|---|
| $25 billion | Faith Flynn | France |
| $26 billion | Nadine Newton | Germany |
| $27 billion | Betty Bush | England |
| $28 billion | Gil Gallegos | Sweden |
| $29 billion | Tim Townsend | Argentina |

# LOGIC PUZZLES

## PUZZLE #6 – SALON APPOINTMENTS

| | | |
|---|---|---|
| 11:00am | Myra | Pam |
| 12:00pm | Alison | Nettie |
| 1:00pm | Cristina | Susie |
| 2:00pm | Blanche | Yvonne |
| 3:00pm | Dolores | Rhonda |

## PUZZLE #7 - BEST IN SHOW

| | | |
|---|---|---|
| 2006 | Barbara | beagle |
| 2007 | Fernando | chow chow |
| 2008 | Douglas | irish setter |
| 2009 | Ginger | dalmatian |
| 2010 | Elsie | great dane |

## PUZZLE #8 – PAM'S PARTY SHOP

| | | | |
|---|---|---|---|
| October 3 | rock band | Ingram | Terrace Avenue |
| October 4 | magician | Garner | Ronald Street |
| October 5 | photo booth | Thornton | Holly Street |
| October 6 | bounce castle | O'Connor | Island Drive |

## PUZZLE #9 – INTERNATIONAL DIPLOMACY

| | | | |
|---|---|---|---|
| January | Pickett | 6 day | Paris |
| February | Nguyen | 9 day | Lisbon |
| March | Underwood | 4 day | Kiev |
| April | Ellison | 7 day | Warsaw |

## PUZZLE #10 - LOTTERY WINNERS

| | | | |
|---|---|---|---|
| $5 million | Cal Chandler | Iowa | teacher |
| $10 million | Ed Elliott | Hawaii | lawyer |
| $15 million | Hilda Hunt | Georgia | banker |
| $20 million | Betty Baxter | Florida | judge |

# MATHDOKU

### PUZZLE #1

| | | | | | |
|---|---|---|---|---|---|
| 9 | × | 1 | + | 8 | = | 17 |
| × | | × | | × | | |
| 6 | × | 3 | − | 2 | = | 16 |
| − | | + | | − | | |
| 7 | + | 5 | + | 4 | = | 16 |
| = | | = | | = | | |
| 47 | | 8 | | 12 | | |

### PUZZLE #2

| | | | | | |
|---|---|---|---|---|---|
| 6 | × | 7 | − | 8 | = | 34 |
| ÷ | | × | | + | | |
| 1 | − | 2 | + | 3 | = | 2 |
| + | | + | | + | | |
| 9 | + | 4 | + | 5 | = | 18 |
| = | | = | | = | | |
| 15 | | 18 | | 16 | | |

### PUZZLE #3

| | | | | | |
|---|---|---|---|---|---|
| 2 | + | 3 | + | 8 | = | 13 |
| + | | − | | × | | |
| 5 | × | 4 | − | 7 | = | 13 |
| + | | + | | + | | |
| 6 | − | 1 | + | 9 | = | 14 |
| = | | = | | = | | |
| 13 | | 0 | | 65 | | |

### PUZZLE #4

| | | | | | |
|---|---|---|---|---|---|
| 6 | ÷ | 3 | + | 2 | = | 4 |
| + | | + | | + | | |
| 7 | + | 9 | + | 8 | = | 24 |
| + | | − | | + | | |
| 5 | + | 1 | − | 4 | = | 2 |
| = | | = | | = | | |
| 18 | | 11 | | 14 | | |

# MATHDOKU

## PUZZLE #5

| 7 | ÷ | 1 | + | 5 | = | 12 |
|---|---|---|---|---|---|----|
| × |   | − |   | + |   |    |
| 3 | + | 2 | − | 4 | = | 1  |
| + |   | + |   | + |   |    |
| 9 | × | 8 | + | 6 | = | 78 |
| = |   | = |   | = |   |    |
| 30 |  | 7 |   | 15 |  |    |

## PUZZLE #6

| 5 | − | 3 | + | 6 | = | 8  |
|---|---|---|---|---|---|----|
| + |   | + |   | × |   |    |
| 9 | × | 7 | + | 8 | = | 71 |
| − |   | + |   | + |   |    |
| 2 | + | 4 | + | 1 | = | 7  |
| = |   | = |   | = |   |    |
| 12 |  | 14 |  | 49 |  |   |

## PUZZLE #7

| 9 | × | 3 | + | 2 | = | 29 |
|---|---|---|---|---|---|----|
| × |   | + |   | × |   |    |
| 7 | + | 5 | + | 6 | = | 18 |
| + |   | − |   | + |   |    |
| 1 | × | 8 | + | 4 | = | 12 |
| = |   | = |   | = |   |    |
| 64 |  | 0 |   | 16 |  |   |

## PUZZLE #8

| 9 | × | 4 | + | 7 | = | 43 |
|---|---|---|---|---|---|----|
| + |   | ÷ |   | + |   |    |
| 6 | ÷ | 2 | − | 3 | = | 0  |
| − |   | + |   | − |   |    |
| 5 | − | 1 | + | 8 | = | 12 |
| = |   | = |   | = |   |    |
| 10 |  | 3 |   | 2 |   |    |

## PUZZLE #9

| 9 | × | 1 | + | 3 | = | 12 |
|---|---|---|---|---|---|----|
| × |   | × |   | + |   |    |
| 6 | − | 4 | + | 8 | = | 10 |
| + |   | + |   | + |   |    |
| 2 | × | 7 | − | 5 | = | 9  |
| = |   | = |   | = |   |    |
| 56 |  | 11 |  | 16 |  |   |

## PUZZLE #10

| 9 | × | 3 | + | 8 | = | 35 |
|---|---|---|---|---|---|----|
| ÷ |   | + |   | + |   |    |
| 1 | × | 2 | + | 5 | = | 7  |
| + |   | − |   | + |   |    |
| 7 | × | 4 | − | 6 | = | 22 |
| = |   | = |   | = |   |    |
| 16 |  | 1 |   | 19 |  |   |

# MAZES

### PUZZLE #1

### PUZZLE #2

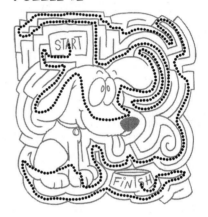

### PUZZLE #3

### PUZZLE #4

# MAZES

### PUZZLE #5

### PUZZLE #6

### PUZZLE #7

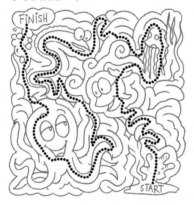

### PUZZLE #8

### PUZZLE #9

### PUZZLE #10

# MORE OR LESS (4X4)

### PUZZLE #1

| 2 | 3 | 1 | 4 |
| 1 | 4 > 3 > 2 |
| 3 | 2 | 4 | 1 |
| 4 | 1 < 2 | 3 |

(∨ below 2 in row1 col1; ∨ below 4 in row3 col3)

### PUZZLE #2

| 4 | 2 | 1 | 3 |
| 2 | 4 > 3 | 1 |
| 1 | 3 | 2 | 4 |
| 3 | 1 | 4 | 2 |

(∧ above 1 in row1 col3; ∨ below 2 in row2 col1)

### PUZZLE #3

| 1 | 4 | 3 | 2 |
| 2 | 3 | 4 | 1 |
| 4 | 2 | 1 | 3 |
| 3 > 1 | 2 | 4 |

(∧ above 1 col1; ∧ above 3 col3; ∨ below 3 col3; ∧ above 2 col3; ∧ above 4 col4)

### PUZZLE #4

| 4 > 2 | 1 | 3 |
| 1 | 3 | 2 < 4 |
| 2 | 4 | 3 | 1 |
| 3 > 1 | 4 | 2 |

(∧ above 1 col3 row1; ∧ above 2 col3 row2; ∧ above 4 col3 row4; ∧ above 2 col4 row4)

### PUZZLE #5

| 2 > 1 | 3 | 4 |
| 3 | 4 | 2 | 1 |
| 1 | 2 | 4 > 3 |
| 4 > 3 | 1 | 2 |

(∨ below 3 col3 row1; ∧ above 3 col4 row3)

### PUZZLE #6

| 3 | 1 | 4 | 2 |
| 2 < 4 | 3 | 1 |
| 1 | 3 > 2 | 4 |
| 4 | 2 | 1 | 3 |

(∧ above 4 col4 row3; ∨ below 2 col3 row3)

### PUZZLE #7

| 2 | 4 | 1 | 3 |
| 1 | 2 | 3 | 4 |
| 4 | 3 | 2 | 1 |
| 3 > 1 | 4 > 2 |

(∨ below 3 col1 row4)

### PUZZLE #8

| 1 | 3 < 4 | 2 |
| 4 | 2 | 1 | 3 |
| 3 | 4 | 2 > 1 |
| 2 | 1 | 3 | 4 |

(∨ below 3 col2 row1; ∧ above 2 col3 row3)

# MORE OR LESS (5X5)

## PUZZLE #1

| 3 < | 4 | 2 | 1 | 5 |
|---|---|---|---|---|
| 2 | 5 | 4 | 3 | 1 |
| 4 | 3 | 1 | 5 | 2 |
| 1 | 2 | 5 | 4 | 3 |
| 5 | 1 | 3 | 2 | 4 |

## PUZZLE #2

| 5 | 1 | 3 | 4 | 2 |
|---|---|---|---|---|
| 2 | 5 > | 4 | 1 | 3 |
| 1 | 2 | 5 | 3 | 4 |
| 3 | 4 > | 2 < | 5 | 1 |
| 4 | 3 | 1 | 2 | 5 |

## PUZZLE #3

| 1 | 5 | 2 | 4 > | 3 |
|---|---|---|---|---|
| 4 | 1 | 3 | 5 | 2 |
| 5 | 3 | 1 | 2 | 4 |
| 3 | 2 | 4 | 1 | 5 |
| 2 | 4 | 5 | 3 > | 1 |

## PUZZLE #4

| 5 | 2 | 4 | 1 | 3 |
|---|---|---|---|---|
| 4 | 5 | 2 | 3 | 1 |
| 2 | 1 | 3 < | 4 < | 5 |
| 1 | 3 | 5 | 2 < | 4 |
| 3 | 4 | 1 | 5 | 2 |

## PUZZLE #5

| 4 < | 5 | 2 | 3 | 1 |
|---|---|---|---|---|
| 3 > | 1 | 5 | 2 | 4 |
| 5 | 3 | 4 | 1 | 2 |
| 1 | 2 | 3 | 4 < | 5 |
| 2 | 4 | 1 | 5 | 3 |

## PUZZLE #6

| 1 | 4 | 3 | 5 | 2 |
|---|---|---|---|---|
| 2 | 3 | 5 | 1 | 4 |
| 3 | 1 | 2 < | 4 | 5 |
| 5 | 2 | 4 | 3 | 1 |
| 4 | 5 | 1 < | 2 | 3 |

# MORSE CODE

# NEIGHBORS (4X4)

### PUZZLE #1

| 3 | 4 | 2 | 1 |
|---|---|---|---|
| 2 | 3 | 1 | 4 |
| 4 | 1 | 3 | 2 |
| 1 | 2 | 4 | 3 |

### PUZZLE #2

| 3 | 1 | 4 | 2 |
|---|---|---|---|
| 1 | 3 | 2 | 4 |
| 2 | 4 | 3 | 1 |
| 4 | 2 | 1 | 3 |

### PUZZLE #3

| 2 | 3 | 1 | 4 |
|---|---|---|---|
| 1 | 4 | 2 | 3 |
| 4 | 2 | 3 | 1 |
| 3 | 1 | 4 | 2 |

### PUZZLE #4

| 3 | 2 | 1 | 4 |
|---|---|---|---|
| 4 | 1 | 2 | 3 |
| 2 | 4 | 3 | 1 |
| 1 | 3 | 4 | 2 |

### PUZZLE #5

| 4 | 2 | 3 | 1 |
|---|---|---|---|
| 3 | 1 | 2 | 4 |
| 1 | 3 | 4 | 2 |
| 2 | 4 | 1 | 3 |

### PUZZLE #6

| 4 | 1 | 2 | 3 |
|---|---|---|---|
| 2 | 3 | 4 | 1 |
| 3 | 4 | 1 | 2 |
| 1 | 2 | 3 | 4 |

### PUZZLE #7

| 4 | 1 | 2 | 3 |
|---|---|---|---|
| 3 | 2 | 4 | 1 |
| 2 | 3 | 1 | 4 |
| 1 | 4 | 3 | 2 |

### PUZZLE #8

| 2 | 3 | 1 | 4 |
|---|---|---|---|
| 3 | 2 | 4 | 1 |
| 4 | 1 | 2 | 3 |
| 1 | 4 | 3 | 2 |

# NEIGHBORS (5X5)

### PUZZLE #1

| 2 | 3 | 4 | 5 | 1 |
| 5 | 4 | 1 | 2 | 3 |
| 3 | 2 | 5 | 1 | 4 |
| 1 | 5 | 3 | 4 | 2 |
| 4 | 1 | 2 | 3 | 5 |

### PUZZLE #2

| 3 | 4 | 2 | 5 | 1 |
| 4 | 3 | 1 | 2 | 5 |
| 2 | 1 | 5 | 4 | 3 |
| 5 | 2 | 3 | 1 | 4 |
| 1 | 5 | 4 | 3 | 2 |

### PUZZLE #3

| 2 | 5 | 3 | 1 | 4 |
| 4 | 2 | 1 | 5 | 3 |
| 1 | 3 | 2 | 4 | 5 |
| 3 | 4 | 5 | 2 | 1 |
| 5 | 1 | 4 | 3 | 2 |

### PUZZLE #4

| 5 | 1 | 3 | 2 | 4 |
| 4 | 3 | 2 | 5 | 1 |
| 2 | 4 | 1 | 3 | 5 |
| 3 | 5 | 4 | 1 | 2 |
| 1 | 2 | 5 | 4 | 3 |

### PUZZLE #5

| 2 | 4 | 3 | 1 | 5 |
| 1 | 5 | 2 | 4 | 3 |
| 4 | 3 | 1 | 5 | 2 |
| 3 | 1 | 5 | 2 | 4 |
| 5 | 2 | 4 | 3 | 1 |

### PUZZLE #6

| 2 | 5 | 3 | 4 | 1 |
| 5 | 4 | 2 | 1 | 3 |
| 3 | 2 | 1 | 5 | 4 |
| 4 | 1 | 5 | 3 | 2 |
| 1 | 3 | 4 | 2 | 5 |

### PUZZLE #7

| 5 | 2 | 1 | 3 | 4 |
| 1 | 4 | 3 | 5 | 2 |
| 4 | 3 | 2 | 1 | 5 |
| 2 | 1 | 5 | 4 | 3 |
| 3 | 5 | 4 | 2 | 1 |

### PUZZLE #8

| 1 | 5 | 4 | 3 | 2 |
| 3 | 4 | 2 | 1 | 5 |
| 4 | 2 | 3 | 5 | 1 |
| 5 | 3 | 1 | 2 | 4 |
| 2 | 1 | 5 | 4 | 3 |

# PATHWAYS (4X4)

**PUZZLE #1**

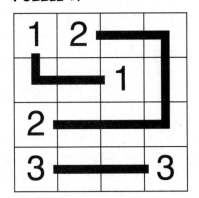

**PUZZLE #2**

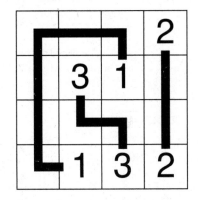

# PATHWAYS (5X5)

### PUZZLE #3

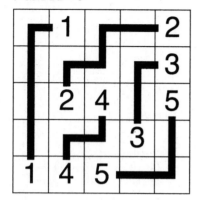

### PUZZLE #4

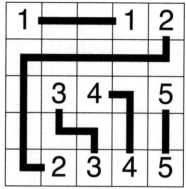

### PUZZLE #5

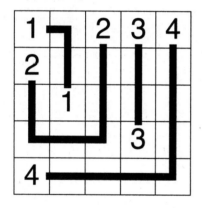

### PUZZLE #6

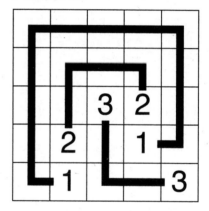

# PATHWAYS (6X6)

### PUZZLE #7

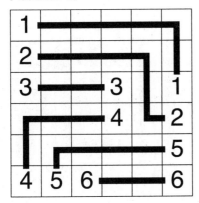

### PUZZLE #8

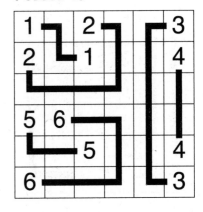

### PUZZLE #9

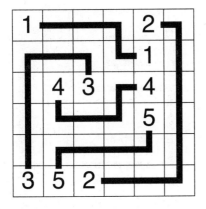

### PUZZLE #10

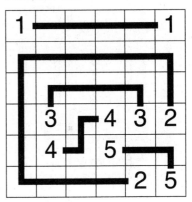

### PUZZLE #11

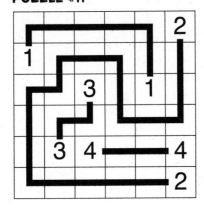

# PATHWAYS (7X7)

### PUZZLE #12

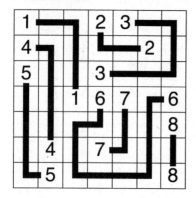

### PUZZLE #13

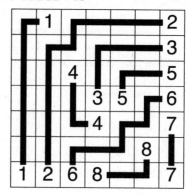

### PUZZLE #14

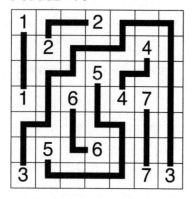

### PUZZLE #15

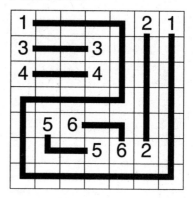

### PUZZLE #16

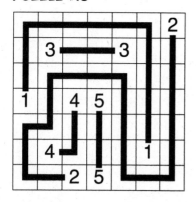

# PATTERN RECOGNITION

**PUZZLE #1**
13
the next odd number

**PUZZLE #2**
32
Each number in the *series* is the previous number multiplied by 2.

**PUZZLE #3**
29
Each number is the sum of the two numbers before it.

**PUZZLE #4**
20
The series is an ordered list of numbers that start with the letter "T".

**PUZZLE #5**
30
Every number in the *series* is the sum of the previous number and either 2 or 7, sequentially.

**PUZZLE #6**
G
The series is in alphabetical order.

**PUZZLE #7**
R
The series is every third letter in the alphabet.

**PUZZLE #8**
DED
Every letter in each three-letter combination is advanced by one, alphabetically.

**PUZZLE #9**
Q
The series is an alphabetical list of capital letters with "closed loops" in their shapes.

**PUZZLE #10**
The next shape in the series is a triangle.
Every shape in the *series* has one fewer side than the one before it.

# REBUS PUZZLES

**PUZZLE #1**
One in a million

**PUZZLE #2**
Man overboard

**PUZZLE #3**
Up for grabs

**PUZZLE #4**
Hop up and down

**PUZZLE #5**
Crossroads

**PUZZLE #6**
Just in time

**PUZZLE #7**
Read between the lines

**PUZZLE #8**
You're under arrest

**PUZZLE #9**
Banana split

**PUZZLE #10**
Backwards glance

**PUZZLE #11**
There are a lot of fish in the sea

**PUZZLE #12**
Holy cow!

**PUZZLE #13**
Right between the eyes

**PUZZLE #14**
Neon lights

**PUZZLE #15**
Stretching the truth

# RHYMING PAIRS

**PUZZLE #1**
CRUEL, POOL
TOOL, STOOL
RULE, SCHOOL

**PUZZLE #2**
EEL, MEAL
FEEL, HEEL
SQUEAL, SEAL

**PUZZLE #3**
ABLE, LABEL
CABLE, TABLE
FABLE, STABLE

**PUZZLE #4**
BEAK, CREEK
SEEK, GREEK
WEEK, PEAK

**PUZZLE #5**
SPEND, MEND
FRIEND, LEND
SEND, BEND

# SCRAMBLERS

**PUZZLE #1**

HAWK
CROW
EAGLE
CARDINAL
FLAMINGO

Q: What is the most expensive bird?
A: The GOLDFINCH!

**PUZZLE #2**

TUNA
SHARK
TROUT
SALMON
SARDINE
FLOUNDER

Q: Why did the crab cross the road?
A: To get to the OTHER TIDE!

# SHARED SEGMENTS

**PUZZLE #1**
COUNT

**PUZZLE #2**
RIGHT

**PUZZLE #3**
RAIN

**PUZZLE #4**
SAND

**PUZZLE #5**
PLAN

**PUZZLE #6**
CAN'T

**PUZZLE #7**
RANG

**PUZZLE #8**
SUM

**PUZZLE #9**
APE

**PUZZLE #10**
BAT

# SUDOKU (4X4)

### PUZZLE #1

| 3 | 4 | 2 | 1 |
|---|---|---|---|
| 2 | 1 | 4 | 3 |
| 4 | 3 | 1 | 2 |
| 1 | 2 | 3 | 4 |

### PUZZLE #2

| 4 | 2 | 3 | 1 |
|---|---|---|---|
| 3 | 1 | 2 | 4 |
| 1 | 3 | 4 | 2 |
| 2 | 4 | 1 | 3 |

### PUZZLE #3

| 2 | 1 | 3 | 4 |
|---|---|---|---|
| 4 | 3 | 1 | 2 |
| 3 | 4 | 2 | 1 |
| 1 | 2 | 4 | 3 |

### PUZZLE #4

| 2 | 4 | 3 | 1 |
|---|---|---|---|
| 3 | 1 | 4 | 2 |
| 1 | 3 | 2 | 4 |
| 4 | 2 | 1 | 3 |

### PUZZLE #5

| 1 | 3 | 4 | 2 |
|---|---|---|---|
| 4 | 2 | 3 | 1 |
| 2 | 4 | 1 | 3 |
| 3 | 1 | 2 | 4 |

### PUZZLE #6

| 2 | 3 | 1 | 4 |
|---|---|---|---|
| 4 | 1 | 3 | 2 |
| 3 | 2 | 4 | 1 |
| 1 | 4 | 2 | 3 |

# SUDOKU (6x6)

### PUZZLE #1

| 4 | 3 | 5 | 2 | 6 | 1 |
|---|---|---|---|---|---|
| 2 | 1 | 6 | 4 | 5 | 3 |
| 6 | 4 | 1 | 5 | 3 | 2 |
| 5 | 2 | 3 | 1 | 4 | 6 |
| 1 | 6 | 4 | 3 | 2 | 5 |
| 3 | 5 | 2 | 6 | 1 | 4 |

### PUZZLE #2

| 3 | 4 | 2 | 5 | 1 | 6 |
|---|---|---|---|---|---|
| 1 | 6 | 5 | 4 | 2 | 3 |
| 6 | 3 | 4 | 1 | 5 | 2 |
| 2 | 5 | 1 | 6 | 3 | 4 |
| 4 | 1 | 3 | 2 | 6 | 5 |
| 5 | 2 | 6 | 3 | 4 | 1 |

### PUZZLE #3

| 1 | 6 | 2 | 3 | 5 | 4 |
|---|---|---|---|---|---|
| 4 | 5 | 3 | 6 | 2 | 1 |
| 6 | 2 | 1 | 4 | 3 | 5 |
| 5 | 3 | 4 | 1 | 6 | 2 |
| 2 | 4 | 6 | 5 | 1 | 3 |
| 3 | 1 | 5 | 2 | 4 | 6 |

### PUZZLE #4

| 5 | 6 | 1 | 4 | 3 | 2 |
|---|---|---|---|---|---|
| 2 | 4 | 3 | 6 | 1 | 5 |
| 1 | 5 | 6 | 3 | 2 | 4 |
| 3 | 2 | 4 | 1 | 5 | 6 |
| 4 | 1 | 2 | 5 | 6 | 3 |
| 6 | 3 | 5 | 2 | 4 | 1 |

### PUZZLE #5

| 1 | 4 | 5 | 3 | 6 | 2 |
|---|---|---|---|---|---|
| 2 | 3 | 6 | 1 | 5 | 4 |
| 6 | 2 | 1 | 5 | 4 | 3 |
| 4 | 5 | 3 | 2 | 1 | 6 |
| 5 | 6 | 2 | 4 | 3 | 1 |
| 3 | 1 | 4 | 6 | 2 | 5 |

### PUZZLE #6

| 6 | 5 | 3 | 2 | 1 | 4 |
|---|---|---|---|---|---|
| 4 | 1 | 2 | 6 | 3 | 5 |
| 1 | 4 | 6 | 5 | 2 | 3 |
| 3 | 2 | 5 | 1 | 4 | 6 |
| 2 | 6 | 4 | 3 | 5 | 1 |
| 5 | 3 | 1 | 4 | 6 | 2 |

### PUZZLE #7

| 2 | 6 | 1 | 3 | 4 | 5 |
|---|---|---|---|---|---|
| 4 | 3 | 5 | 1 | 2 | 6 |
| 6 | 1 | 4 | 5 | 3 | 2 |
| 3 | 5 | 2 | 4 | 6 | 1 |
| 5 | 4 | 6 | 2 | 1 | 3 |
| 1 | 2 | 3 | 6 | 5 | 4 |

### PUZZLE #8

| 6 | 2 | 5 | 3 | 4 | 1 |
|---|---|---|---|---|---|
| 4 | 3 | 1 | 2 | 6 | 5 |
| 5 | 4 | 2 | 6 | 1 | 3 |
| 1 | 6 | 3 | 5 | 2 | 4 |
| 2 | 5 | 4 | 1 | 3 | 6 |
| 3 | 1 | 6 | 4 | 5 | 2 |

### PUZZLE #9

| 1 | 5 | 2 | 6 | 4 | 3 |
|---|---|---|---|---|---|
| 6 | 3 | 4 | 5 | 1 | 2 |
| 2 | 1 | 6 | 3 | 5 | 4 |
| 3 | 4 | 5 | 2 | 6 | 1 |
| 5 | 2 | 1 | 4 | 3 | 6 |
| 4 | 6 | 3 | 1 | 2 | 5 |

### PUZZLE #10

| 5 | 6 | 1 | 4 | 2 | 3 |
|---|---|---|---|---|---|
| 4 | 3 | 2 | 6 | 1 | 5 |
| 6 | 2 | 4 | 5 | 3 | 1 |
| 3 | 1 | 5 | 2 | 6 | 4 |
| 2 | 4 | 3 | 1 | 5 | 6 |
| 1 | 5 | 6 | 3 | 4 | 2 |

# SUDOKU (9X9)

## PUZZLE #1

| 8 | 6 | 2 | 3 | 4 | 7 | 5 | 1 | 9 |
| 3 | 7 | 4 | 5 | 9 | 1 | 8 | 6 | 2 |
| 1 | 9 | 5 | 2 | 8 | 6 | 7 | 3 | 4 |
| 6 | 4 | 8 | 7 | 3 | 9 | 2 | 5 | 1 |
| 9 | 5 | 7 | 1 | 6 | 2 | 4 | 8 | 3 |
| 2 | 3 | 1 | 8 | 5 | 4 | 9 | 7 | 6 |
| 5 | 2 | 9 | 6 | 1 | 8 | 3 | 4 | 7 |
| 7 | 1 | 3 | 4 | 2 | 5 | 6 | 9 | 8 |
| 4 | 8 | 6 | 9 | 7 | 3 | 1 | 2 | 5 |

## PUZZLE #2

| 4 | 9 | 2 | 3 | 6 | 7 | 1 | 5 | 8 |
| 8 | 1 | 5 | 4 | 2 | 9 | 7 | 6 | 3 |
| 6 | 3 | 7 | 1 | 5 | 8 | 4 | 2 | 9 |
| 9 | 5 | 8 | 6 | 7 | 1 | 2 | 3 | 4 |
| 1 | 4 | 6 | 5 | 3 | 2 | 8 | 9 | 7 |
| 7 | 2 | 3 | 8 | 9 | 4 | 6 | 1 | 5 |
| 5 | 8 | 9 | 2 | 4 | 6 | 3 | 7 | 1 |
| 2 | 7 | 4 | 9 | 1 | 3 | 5 | 8 | 6 |
| 3 | 6 | 1 | 7 | 8 | 5 | 9 | 4 | 2 |

## PUZZLE #3

| 5 | 2 | 7 | 8 | 1 | 6 | 3 | 4 | 9 |
| 4 | 8 | 6 | 3 | 9 | 5 | 7 | 2 | 1 |
| 3 | 1 | 9 | 2 | 7 | 4 | 5 | 8 | 6 |
| 8 | 6 | 2 | 4 | 3 | 1 | 9 | 5 | 7 |
| 7 | 3 | 5 | 6 | 2 | 9 | 8 | 1 | 4 |
| 1 | 9 | 4 | 5 | 8 | 7 | 2 | 6 | 3 |
| 6 | 4 | 3 | 9 | 5 | 8 | 1 | 7 | 2 |
| 9 | 7 | 8 | 1 | 4 | 2 | 6 | 3 | 5 |
| 2 | 5 | 1 | 7 | 6 | 3 | 4 | 9 | 8 |

## PUZZLE #4

| 8 | 3 | 5 | 9 | 4 | 2 | 7 | 1 | 6 |
| 9 | 6 | 7 | 1 | 5 | 8 | 3 | 4 | 2 |
| 4 | 2 | 1 | 3 | 7 | 6 | 9 | 5 | 8 |
| 2 | 4 | 9 | 8 | 1 | 7 | 6 | 3 | 5 |
| 1 | 8 | 6 | 2 | 3 | 5 | 4 | 9 | 7 |
| 5 | 7 | 3 | 6 | 9 | 4 | 2 | 8 | 1 |
| 6 | 5 | 4 | 7 | 8 | 3 | 1 | 2 | 9 |
| 3 | 9 | 2 | 5 | 6 | 1 | 8 | 7 | 4 |
| 7 | 1 | 8 | 4 | 2 | 9 | 5 | 6 | 3 |

# TELEPHONE

**PUZZLE #1**

To get to the other slide.

**PUZZLE #2**

Because seven ate nine.

**PUZZLE #3**

He stole the show.

**PUZZLE #4**

They have webbed feet.

**PUZZLE #5**

A lost elephant.

**PUZZLE #6**

You are looking sharp.

**PUZZLE #7**

In case they get a hole in one.

**PUZZLE #8**

A postage stamp.

**PUZZLE #9**

In a snowbank.

**PUZZLE #10**

He knew it was pointless.

# VOWELLESS

**PUZZLE #1**
Snake
Crocodile
Lizard
Alligator
Iguana

**PUZZLE #2**
France
Canada
Mexico
Italy
India

**PUZZLE #3**
Washington
Lincoln
Kennedy
Eisenhower
Adams

**PUZZLE #4**
Green
Yellow
Violet
Orange
Indigo

**PUZZLE #5**
Broccoli
Carrot
Eggplant
Potato
Onion

**PUZZLE #6**
Silver
Copper
Bronze
Titanium
Iron

**PUZZLE #7**
Squirrel
Beaver
Walrus
Elephant
Otter

**PUZZLE #8**
January
June
October
April
August

**PUZZLE #9**
Large
Gigantic
Huge
Enormous
Immense

**PUZZLE #10**
Jupiter
Mercury
Neptune
Earth
Uranus

# WORD BLOCKS

**PUZZLE #1**
ANECDOTES
DEVELOPED
REMAINDER
COMMITTEE
CONSIDERS
ADVISABLE

**PUZZLE #2**
CHOCOLATE
CONDUCTOR
SWITCHING
INSTALLED
AFTERNOON
NETWORKED

**PUZZLE #3**
SEARCHING
ECCENTRIC
COLLAPSED
PERMANENT
CONCEALED
APOLOGIES

**PUZZLE #4**
FULFILLED
DISHONEST
DIMENSION
APPEALING
DETERMINE
SENTIMENT

**PUZZLE #5**
VARIABLES
ALONGSIDE
ADMISSION
CURRENTLY
PRESIDENT
HOSPITALS

**PUZZLE #6**
LANDSCAPE
HIERARCHY
ATTACHING
DELIVERED
AMUSEMENT
HAPPINESS

**PUZZLE #7**
EXCELLENT
ACCORDING
HOPEFULLY
CHEMISTRY
ANNOUNCED
IMPORTANT

**PUZZLE #8**
ABANDONED
BLACKMAIL
EMPLOYEES
ATTENTION
CUSTOMERS
PORTRAYED

**PUZZLE #9**
DISCOVERS
GRADUALLY
STRETCHED
SUSPENDED
INTRODUCE
ADVENTURE

**PUZZLE #10**
CONFIRMED
CHALLENGE
POLICEMAN
SPOKESMAN
FORTUNATE
EVERYBODY

# WORD LADDERS

**PUZZLE #1**
SELL
FELL
FALL

**PUZZLE #2**
DOVE
DIVE
DIME

**PUZZLE #3**
TUNA
TUNE
TONE

**PUZZLE #4**
PANT
PINT
PINE

**PUZZLE #5**
BEAR
BEAT
BEET

**PUZZLE #6**
GOATS
BOATS
BOOTS

**PUZZLE #7**
FAIRY
FAIRS
FAILS

**PUZZLE #8**
BUTTER
BATTER
MATTER

**PUZZLE #9**
BOXES
BONES
CONES

**PUZZLE #10**
WHILE
WHINE
SHINE

# WORD SEARCH

## PUZZLE #1

```
N A N A N N B A A N B
A B N N A A A A B N N
A A A B A B N N A A B
N A B N B A B A A N A
A N N B A N A B B A N
A B A A A A B A N B N
N A A N B N B A A N A
B B A B A B A B N A N
N A N A B N A N A N B
B N A N A A N A A B A
N B N N A B A A B A N
```

## PUZZLE #2

```
H K E V R R S B O P K
Y E V D J E Y I A I T
L N I I V T W X H N
A I F L R B W O R F U
H N E U X L T E V I G
W W I O S W E J N F Y
T Y R U O F C V T T V
N E V E L E S O R V Y
M H B I E S N O L R G
Y T H G I E F N E T C
B C N E E T R I H T Y
```

## PUZZLE #3

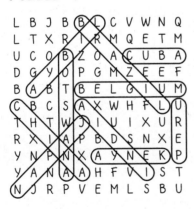

```
L B J B B L C V W N Q
L T X R I R M Q E T M
U C O B Z O A C U B A
D G Y O P G M Z E E F
B A B T B E L G I U M
C B C S A X W H F L U
T H T W J I U I X U R
R X I A P B D S N X E
Y N P N X A Y N E K P
Y A N A A H F V I S T
N J R P V E M L S B U
```

## PUZZLE #4

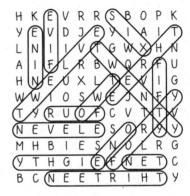

```
Y K L T W L M E G
S C Y B E K I V
N E D R S M R P M
A G R E X A I I H
W F I E F C Y G E
E F B D K S S T
Z I E W Y I U P Q
O I S C G Y O P N O
I H J M M A K S P
```

# WORD SEARCH

### PUZZLE #5

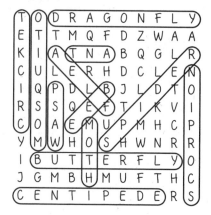

### PUZZLE #6

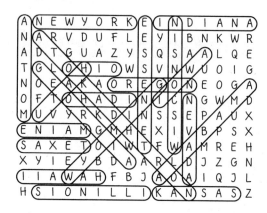

### PUZZLE #7

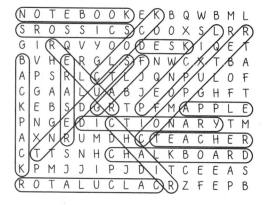

### PUZZLE #8

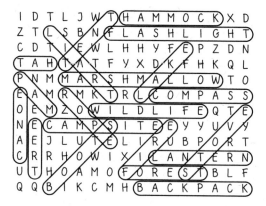

### PUZZLE #9

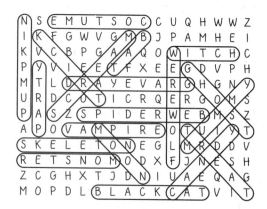

### PUZZLE #10

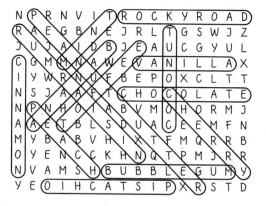

# WORDS OUT OF WORDS

**PUZZLE #1**
HORSE
COINS
OREOS
INCHES
CORNER

**PUZZLE #2**
ERUPT
ACTOR
ERASE
SAUCER
COASTER

**PUZZLE #3**
STONE
STEAM
MANES
TENNIS
MANSION

**PUZZLE #4**
TREAT
HEART
MARCH
EARTH
HERMIT

**PUZZLE #5**
BEARS
NURSE
BRAIN
NUMBER
BRUISE

**PUZZLE #6**
PIANO
PILOT
PARENT
TRIPLE
PLANET

**PUZZLE #7**
GREEN
TIGER
GENIE
ENGINE
INTEGER

**PUZZLE #8**
AUNTS
SHARP
HABIT
SPRINT
PUNISH

**PUZZLE #9**
GUILT
GOLDEN
TONGUE
UNITED
TOILED

**PUZZLE #10**
ALARM
DREAM
MEDAL
SALAD
SANDAL